ONE TO ONE

ONE TO ONE

UNDERSTANDING
PERSONAL RELATIONSHIPS

Theodore Isaac Rubin, M.D.

A TOM DOHERTY ASSOCIATES BOOK

NEW YORK

ONE TO ONE

This book was originally published in 1983 by the Viking Press.

A Forge Book
Published by Tom Doherty Associates, LLC
175 Fifth Avenue
New York, NY 10010

Forge® is a registered trademark of Tom Doherty Associates, LLC

Designed by Lisa Pifher

Library of Congress Cataloging-in-Publication Data

Rubin, Theodore Isaac.
    One to one : understanding personal relationships / Theodore Isaac
Rubin. — 1st ed.
        p.   cm.
    ISBN 0-312-87184-8 (acid-free paper)
    1. Interpersonal relations.   2. Interpersonal relations Case
studies.   I. Title.
HM1106.R82   1999
302–dc21   99-21604
                                                                          CIP

First Forge Edition: August 1999

Printed in the United States of America

0   9   8   7   6   5   4   3   2   1

To our children,
who teach us forgiveness.
We forgive them no matter what,
and in so doing we learn to forgive
ourselves and each other. Should we
stop forgiving them,
we are lost.

CONTENTS

IV SOCIETY AND CULTURE

V THE CURRENCY OF RELATING

VI   AFFECTIVE RELATING

VII   EPILOGUE: A SUGGESTED THERAPEUTIC GAME

ACKNOWLEDGMENTS

I want to thank Ellie, my wife, for providing the opportunity of these many years of creative relating—and for her help in the preparation of this book. My thanks as well to Amanda Vaill, my brilliant editor, for the hard but rewarding work that brought this book into its current form—and thanks to her daughter, Pamela Stewart, whose birth brought several weeks of welcome relief when we most needed it.

PREFACE

When one of my patients comes to me and says he or she is having trouble with a relationship—whether it is at work or in love, at home or outside—I ask four questions:

1. *Do you want a relationship with this other person?* It is, of course, possible that neither party to the relationship really wants it to continue, in which case prolonging the association can be a painful waste of time, or that only one party wants to make it work, in which case the relationship has little chance of success.

2. *Do you want exclusivity in this relationship?* If one relating partner wants an exclusive relationship with the other, but the other partner doesn't, there's bound to be trouble. If neither wants exclusivity, or if both do, there should be no problem.

3. *What has the relationship been like up to now?* Here I want an honest, candid picture of how each partner has related to the other, what each has expected from the other, what each has exacted from the other. And I want to know how each feels about the relationship.

4. *What do you want it to be like?* Here again, specifics are what I am after—not vague, idealized pictures of a dream relationship, but actual expectations, feelings, transactions.

Finally, I ask my patient, or patients, How will we go about getting from 3 to 4? That is what this book is about.

We are relating beings. Indeed, for our species we may almost say that to be is to relate. From the earliest times in our lives, we develop and sustain feelings about ourselves and other people. Sometimes we are in touch with these feelings. Sometimes we distort them, and there are times we are not in touch with them at all. There are also times when we share what we feel about ourselves and one another. These feelings, and the way we share them (or don't share them), determine the nature of our relationships.

The intensity and quality of relationships are dictated largely by the character structures of the participants. These patterns sometimes change in response to the relationships themselves or to the influence of unpredictable outside forces, but such changes are seldom profound or permanent. This is the result of the relatively fixed nature of the character structure of each participant and the tenacity of interpersonal transactions once they become established and familiar.

Nevertheless, human beings often act in totally untoward, unforeseen ways, probably because we repress feelings, desires, and needs that on an unconscious level dictate acts for which the individual seems to possess no discernible potential.

All human beings are infinitely complex. It follows that relationships involving two or more people present possibilities for complexity and complication and unpredictability in geometric proportion.

There is no pure form of relating behavior. Each relationship, however destructive or constructive, contains at least some elements of all relating patterns. It is therefore not unusual to find elements of extreme cruelty in relationships replete with kindness, or elements of kindness in relationships characterized mainly by extreme emotional sadomasochism.

Most people have little or no conscious awareness of how they relate. Many form relationships with little or no conscious choice. Autonomy and control seldom play significant roles in relationships; for the most part, our relationships are influenced by *unconscious* forces.

We relate because we must. This is in the nature of our species. Prolonged isolation often produces imaginary relationships. Very young children, especially those who have no siblings or other playmates, sometimes create phantom friends who accompany them for years. Other people, deprived of all human contact over long periods of time, may develop psychoses, including visual and auditory hallucinations.

Tragically, many human relationships are destructive and painful, rather than supportive and sustaining. Too often the people involved cannot extricate themselves from such a relationship; or if they can, they compulsively and repeatedly form similarly destructive relationships. Too many relationships are characterized by breakdown in communication, mutual emotional and sometimes physical assault, frustrated yearnings, internal loneliness, boredom, and self- and mutual hatred.

If such destructive relationships are the rule between individuals in a society, then certainly the society these units compose must suffer the consequences of these malignancies: aggression, war, plundering of resources, mass persecution, sociopathic institutions. People must relate, but those who relate morbidly form morbid societies.

On the other hand, people who relate constructively have no desire to deprive, to suppress, or to harm anyone else. They tend to form cooperatives that in turn encourage and enhance cooperative relating on the individual level.

I sometimes listen to our world leaders, including those speaking at United Nations forums. Sick pride, malignant competition, the need for self-glorification and vindictive triumph are almost constantly evident in their speeches. These qualities are even more apparent in televised sermons by self-aggrandizing clergymen speaking from diverse religious pulpits. The therapeutic effect of real humility has escaped them completely. To expect constructive, cooperative leadership and help from these sources can only increase our feelings of cynicism and hopelessness.

We must look to ourselves and to our own "small relationships." We must increasingly understand these core relationships if we wish to remedy a very sick society.

In this book I attempt to increase our understanding of how we relate. Relating brings out the best in us, and it brings out the worst. The true depth and scope of our emotional well-being are revealed when we relate. Learning more about ourselves, our individual psychologies and intrapsychic lives, is inevitable in this investigation. Indeed, some discussion of individual character structure is mandatory in our understanding of relating psychology. But our prime focus here is the relating unit, and revelation on an individual level is a secondary benefit.

As I stated earlier, predictions involving human behavior are only sometimes possible. However, through understanding, change and growth are always possible whatever our age or condition.

Theodore Isaac Rubin
Evian, France
August 12, 1980

I

FUNDAMENTALS

THE RELATING PROCESS

Relationships begin when feelings between two people start to evolve and end when feelings stop. Obviously, this can often happen even before two people meet. Hearing about someone else is often enough to generate feelings of one kind or another; a glance is sometimes enough. Relationships can continue even if two people no longer see each other, as long as mutual feelings are sustained.

Relationships are constituted of all kinds of needs, fantasies, desires, attractions, and other factors, including looks, humor, particular character traits, and much more. These may seem attractive—in which case they will cement the relationship—or they may generate a revulsion that causes the relationship to end, either at its inception, or later on.

The Evolving Relationship

There is no such thing as a status quo in relating. Indeed, there is really no such thing as a *relationship*. We use this term much as we analyze a drop of water in a river to better understand the river as a whole. But in actuality the prime characteristic of a river is that it flows. Otherwise it would be a pond. The same is true of what goes on between people. Feelings flow, feelings are invested, feelings are withdrawn, reactions take place.

In short, we are dealing with a process, an ever-changing process whose dynamics and identifying patterns may remain fairly constant. We are interested in these dynamics and patterns, and that is what this book is all about. Understanding the dynamics and patterns is like understanding the source and destination of the river, the movement of the water and its contents. Like the river, the relating is in flow, ever moving and ever developing. As with the river, if the process stops, relating is over also.

Inertia is a very important characteristic of the relating process: the patterns of particular relationships tend to resist change once they become established. Inasmuch as process connotes change, this seems contradictory, but it isn't. Counterproductive relating gets increasingly damaging as the relationship matures; cooperative, constructive relating tends to become increasingly productive. Sadomasochistic relating tends to become increasingly intricate and devious as it becomes even more sadomasochistic. Such relationships, for the most part, retain their qualitative *character*, but the *intensity* of the process changes.

However, the inertia of the relating process can be changed, too. This sometimes happens as the result of unforeseen events—changes in family status quo, death, illness, career moves, even changes in mood—or because one of the partners in the relationship has changed.

While each of us tends to relate in certain characteristic ways, every relationship we form with each new human being initiates a different kind of relating. Different facets of ourselves come into action in different encounters. Often these different facets are brought to light by hidden memories of the past: people in the present unconsciously remind us of feelings we had about people and events in the past. So no two relationships are alike; they call forth different aspects of ourselves even if the principal patterns remain intact enough to be discernible.

People who are extremely anxious and neurotic tend to be more fixed in the way they relate and are capable of less flexibility and less change. Although it is possible for change to take place in a relationship too rapidly—which indicates instability, fragmentation, and lack of a central, integrated, identifying personality core on the part of the participants—healthy people have the capacity to accommodate or to adjust to the needs of different relationships and moods. They still feel they are the *same people*, even though various aspects of themselves come into play to various degrees in different relationships.

Individuality and Arrhythmia

We must view relating, then, as *what goes on between two people in process*—or, if you will, what goes on between two people who are constantly changing. Human relationship describes the history of two human processes as the individuals interact with each other. As people, we invariably are more alike than different. But no two people are identical—not even identical twins. Each of us is a separate and different person, as unique as our individual fingerprints. Each of us has different requirements for food, sleep, and exercise, and different characteristics of metabolism, aging, growth, disease resistance; these differences overlap into the emotional areas of our lives, too. But it is our emotional physiology that guarantees that no two people will ever feel exactly the same way; our interests, desires, emphases, passions, involvements—everything we know that may come under the broad umbrella of what we call moods and feelings—are always unique.

In addition, our needs, yearnings, desires, feelings, and moods—anything that characterizes our emotional lives and character structures—are in a constant state of flux. This means that not only are we unique but we are constantly *changing* in a unique way. Life is not static. Our emotional lives are certainly not static. We are always in process. The rate of change and the quality of change are also different for each of us. This makes for an infinite variety of emotional rhythms, no two of which are ever alike.

What I am saying here is that not only are we emotionally arrhythmic in terms of one another; we are also arrhythmic in terms of ourselves. We never have exactly the same mood or feelings or emotional set or outlook twice, and of course we never share the same exact state of feelings with anyone at any time either. Yet a great many relationships are characterized mainly by the attempt to make that which is naturally arrhythmic rhythmic. And sympathy, empathy, the healthy motivation to understand one another, to build common interests, to extend a common language, to be more open, tender, and intimate with one another—these are all bastardized in the attempt to obliterate arrhythmia and replace it with rhythmic relating.

Close partners do meet in cooperative concert many times in the course of their relating lives. This occurs in tastes and decisions regarding various issues, beliefs, life's demands, responsibilities, desires, and yearnings. They meet sexually, even though the ebb and flow of their desires are rarely if ever perfectly synchronized. Their view of themselves, of each other, and of their relationship is a relatively compassionate one; it excludes a drive for perfect synchronization—it does not say, "If we loved each other, we would have the same viewpoints and desires at the same time." For the partners know that perfect synchronization and identical rhythms are not necessary for cooperative function. Neither partner makes claims on the other for self-sacrifice in the service of immature definitions of love; neither asks the other to eradicate his or her personal characteristics.

There is little more destructive to individuality and to the relating process than the quest for perfect rhythm or synchronization.

In this quest a two-headed monster is produced that destroys the integrity and the natural rhythms of both selves. We each need a self, a strong and real self, with which to relate, but when a relationship demands perfect synchronization, the extended self of the exploiter is spread thin, leaving little except the continued need to exploit, and the obliterated self of the morbidly dependent, self-effacing martyr winds up as a mirror image of the other partner.

Our culture periodically extols the virtues of "togetherness," even as it periodically extols the virtues of complete independence. But obsessive togetherness or obsessive independence each make for internal conflict, much anxiety, and a destructive relationship.

Mutual dependency is an integral part of the human condition and is a cornerstone of cooperative relating. Relative independence is an extension of a high degree of real self-development, indicating a strong sense of identity, good self-esteem, and a solid feel of personal values and priorities. People of real relative independence enjoy healthy relative mutual dependency and are not threatened by the possibility of emotional depletion, nor do they tend to be exploitative. Carried to extremes, morbid mutual dependency leads to paralyzing crippling of all concerned. Morbid independence leads to paranoid isolation and destructive reclusiveness. If both are present at the same time in the same individual or individuals, severe internal conflict ensues, causing great anxiety. The response to anxiety is to cling to and to run from one another at the same time, producing chaos and still more anxiety.

Origins of Individual Relating Patterns

Each of us tends to relate in particular ways—even though every relationship we have is different. What are the patterns that govern our different relationships? How do these patterns evolve? In this chapter I want to outline briefly ten of the most powerful forces that influence the ways we relate.

1. GENETIC ENDOWMENT

   Our metabolic rates, and perhaps to some degree our temperament, moods, and feelings, are governed—at least in part—by our endocrine glands. And the intensity with which these hormone-secreting structures affect us may be determined by our heredity. Size and looks are also in part genetically determined, and these too play a role in relating, varying in one way or another from culture to culture. State of health may also fit into this category. Intelligence potential and inherent skills and talents have some genetic basis and certainly play a significant role in the relating process.

2. BIRTH ORDER AND FAMILY CIRCUMSTANCES

   Where we are born relative to other children in the family, or whether or not we are the only child, has great relevance in early relating experiences.

   Each child is born into a different environment—other siblings are already there or aren't there when he or she arrives. A child early in his life may sense that an older sibling has already taken on the role of dominance and mastery, and he may react by becoming the self-effacing child in the family.

   Additionally, the state of affairs, emotionally, sexually, socially, and economically, at the time of birth and early childhood has a profound effect. The family's attitude regarding the entry of a new family member at a given time also has far-reaching implications in terms of how one relates to people all of one's life.

3. THE FAMILY'S MYSTIQUE OR SELF-IMAGE

   Does the family view itself as commonplace and prosaic? Is it conventional and establishment-oriented? Does it see itself as being unique and special? Does it feel noble and privileged in some way—a kind of royal mood that prevails? Does it see itself as somehow unlucky, abused, singled out for martyrdom and impoverishment? Is the family cohesive and, above all, loyal to its members? Is it a family of enemies? Is it a group of loosely scattered, almost unrelated people?

Obviously, the family view of itself affects all its members and how they will relate to other people all their lives. This is just as true even if no word is ever spoken about these feelings, so that they exist on a totally unconscious level.

4. THE FAMILY'S ATTITUDE TOWARD THE CHILD

Was he or she overprotected? Were the parents permissive to the point of neglect? Was he brutalized? Overindulged? Was there a lack of confidence in the child? Was he treated in a warm, nurturing way? Were her parents perfectionistic in their expectations of her? Did they share his joys, struggles, and accomplishments? Were they tuned into her needs, assets, limitations, proclivities, and talents? Were friendships encouraged? Did they demonstrate confidence in his growing ability to take care of himself?

5. INTRAFAMILY RELATIONSHIPS

How were the boys and men treated? The girls and women? How did the parents treat each other? The parental model of cooperative or antagonistic relating is often repeated by the child in later life. Was there an emotional vacuum—cold, noninvolved, austere? Were people free to vent their feelings and to exchange ideas and information? Could they readily express love, anger, tears, loudly and quietly, too? Were members permitted privacy? What was the attitude toward one's body, biological function, and sex? Did family members like one another? Were they cooperative or competitive? Was sibling friendship or rivalry encouraged? Did the family socialize with other people? What was their attitude toward nonfamily members?

6. THE INDIVIDUAL'S ATTITUDE TOWARD THE FAMILY

How he or she related to his parents—as a team and individually—is of crucial importance, as are memories of how he felt about siblings or family happenings. It is not important whether these memories are perfectly accurate or not. The fact that he feels the way he does about them influences his present-day relationships.

7. FAMILY MESSAGES ABOUT THE SURROUNDING SOCIETY OR CULTURE

These include feelings, opinions, ideas about friends, other relatives, strangers, entertainment, politics, sports, religion, money, notoriety, philosophies of life. Is the message about other people trusting? Or does the family feel it's a jungle out there? Are people essentially good? Is life hell? Is life a potential heaven on earth—all you've got to do is get the money to unlock the gate and enter? Does everybody exploit everyone else? Are people fun?

8. THE INDIVIDUAL'S UNIQUE LIFE EXPERIENCES

Some of these will be largely generated by him/her. Some will be largely a function of chance and uncontrollable events or happenings. Some of these experiences will dilute early family influences. Others will reinforce or magnify early family influences and effects.

9. HEALTH

The degree of relative health—emotionally and physically— of the family of the person in question and of the individual as a child and as a developing adult is significant.

10. CULTURE AND ENVIRONMENT

The culture a child and his or her family lived in during the child's formative years has great relevance. It can tell us how to relate ("Never trust a stranger," "A woman is so-and-so," "A man is so-and-so"). Obviously, culture and environments change. For example, the influences exerted on families in Japan prior to World War II were quite different from those exerted on families and on children born following World War II. Pre-television birth and development were different from post-television. The culture has profound influence and transmits that influence—whether beneficial or malignant—to children directly and through older family members. The culture and its values are always in a state of flux and always combine health and sickness in ratio. That ratio—and many influences that will affect our relating lives— are factors over which we have no control. If families are healthy, retain considerable spontaneity and their own values, destructive cultural influence will be diluted somewhat. If a family is alienated from feelings and compulsively conforming (or rebellious), the cultural impact will be much more significant.

The Question of Transference

The effect of these early influences and memories on our here-and-now relationships is what analysts refer to when they talk about transferences.* For my purpose here, *transference* refers to transferring feelings for parents and siblings developed early in life to people with whom we relate when we are older.

Does this mean that all adult relationships are only recapitulations of earlier relationships (with parents and siblings), which we are condemned to repeat over and over again? I believe the answer is yes and no.

---

*Some analysts fervently believe in transference neurosis. They think the relationship that evolves between patient and therapist is always a recapitulation of the unresolved neurotic relationships the patient had with parents and siblings. A large part of the analysis consists of understanding the analytic relationship or transference neurosis and resolving the conflicts and problems therein contained. This frees the patient from early relating problems still active in the unconscious, and makes it possible for the patient to pursue healthier relationships relatively free of neurotic residual influences of sick relating to parents.

We bring our total selves into a relationship. Our total selves include those experiences and unresolved feelings still alive in us that we tend to displace to people in our current life. In transference, we confuse current people with past people and prejudice our relationships with old, residual feelings. And in an attempt to remedy old hurts and needs, many of us assign the role of mother, father, brother, sister, wife, or husband, and combinations of all these, to our partner in a relationship. If we have repressed these unresolved conflicts and feelings about parents and siblings, and are therefore out of touch with them, we will unwittingly play out those old relationships with other people repeatedly. This unfinished business, of which we know little or nothing consciously, will largely dictate our relating behavior.

Those of us who believe that what is swept under the carpet doesn't bother us do not understand how powerful the unconscious is. It is precisely that which is unconscious that creates anxiety, depression, phobias, and disastrous relating experiences. The work of psychoanalysis is to make that which is unconscious conscious, or to release the repressed so that it can be handled in the full light of consciousness—to help us find out what it is that is bothering us so that we can change it. This is especially true of destructive relationships that are used to play out old scenes in an unconscious attempt to settle old emotional business.

Each new relationship, if it is a constructive one, can to some extent clear old muddied waters. And so while patterns of relating can be influenced by the past, the present can help to establish *new* patterns. This can happen unconsciously, as when cynicism about the opposite sex, engendered by past experience, is diluted by current good experiences. Or it can happen consciously, through recollection and analysis, when by knowing what bothers us we can do something about it. Thus, at least to some extent, healthy relating may replace sick relating. The potential is there, whether or not there are professional treatment encounters.

Finally, I believe that transferences can also involve the bringing of healthy, spontaneous aspects of ourselves into our current relationships. In short, all of us are subject to both assaults and gifts from the past, but we are not totally trapped. Each new relationship is not simply a psychodrama based on an old play. It is that in part—but it is more.

CHARACTER TYPES

A relationship is no more and no less than the people who compose it, and perhaps the single greatest influence on how people relate is the anatomy of their own character structure. Karen Horney described three main character types, and we will say here that an individual belongs to one type or another. But it is important to keep in mind that purity does not exist in such classifications—each of us is a mixture of the three types. However, one type is usually dominant and largely determines our behavior, especially our relating behavior.

The following is a brief outline of the three types:

People Who Move Toward People

These are self-effacing, compliant people who see love as being of prime importance in their lives. They need to be liked and to be thought of as helpful and nice. They tend to be self-effacing and to have difficulty with turbulence, self-assertion, saying "no," and anger.

In their unconscious idealizations, they see themselves as self-less, self-sacrificing, caring about others above self, being unusually kind, loving, and helpful.

They do poorly alone and tend to be dependent. The major claim made by these people is to be considered lovable no matter what. They are terrified of anger, since anger may result in loss of love. They tend to form severely dependent relationships in which they look for a strong partner from whom to take on strength and sustenance. They are therefore highly susceptible to sadism and usually interpret it as strength. Girl children in our society are much more likely to be pushed into dependency roles than are boy children, incidentally.

Shirley, Frank, and Wally

Shirley and Frank were married about three years and "doing just fine" (they said) until Wally was born.

Things began to go downhill after Shirley gave birth. At first it was subtle, "hardly noticeable." They were both "just irritated with each other more than usually." But they started to fight more and more. By the time Wally was eight, they felt they had a serious problem on their hands, and their fights took on increased bitterness as time went on.

Now Wally, who is a very bright child, is doing poorly in school. His work does not reflect his lively mind and intelligence, and his classmates stay away from him. From their remarks, it is apparent that his classmates and his teachers find him overbearing, arrogant, and altogether abrasive. His teachers also indicate that Wally "seems confused about who he really is—acts like a pedantic little old man instead of like a happy eight-year-old child."

Shirley and Frank are also upset about a few of their very close friends' reaction to Wally. What it boils down to is that he simply isn't liked. Indeed, Shirley's best and oldest friend, Roz, is embarrassed because she has "never disliked a child in my life." Besides, she loves Shirley very much and likes Frank, too. She describes Wally, in essence, as "acting much older than his age," and she resents his "treating adults in a superior sassy way." Roz feels that Wally is highly manipulative and that his parents are "absolute patsys."

Shirley and Frank are serious, intelligent people and "totally family-oriented." They are sure they "love each other and Wally," and *love* means a great deal to them. They are thoroughly confused by what has been happening and can't understand how things have gotten to this point.

Successive interviews provided some elucidation. Shirley and Frank are essentially compliant people. As children they each had a history of being the "good child" who never gave parents any trouble. Neither can remember any display of anger at his or her parents or, for that matter, a display of anger at anybody or anything. They were both very obedient in school, did everything expected of them, and were much liked by teachers and fellow pupils when they were Wally's age. They never permitted themselves to feel—let alone to express—irritation of any kind.

In Wally, they have a superb representative to act out repressed resentment, anger, and rebelliousness against authority, remembered and current. If Wally is the one who shows aggressive behavior toward their friends, they themselves can preserve their own unruffled and unassertive relationships with those friends, however much they may disagree with or be irritated by them.

All this is possible, I believe, because an interesting and thoroughly unconscious transposition has taken place. Shirley and Frank, in their self-effacing zeal to relinquish authority and to be nonassertive, have become childlike; they have made eight-year-old Wally an adult. Their extreme, compulsive overpermissiveness and inability to set limits and boundaries for him have made Wally insecure, manipulative, arrogant, and confused.

Emotionally, he really doesn't know who are the children and who are the parents. Shirley and Frank have transferred their childhood training—their need to be best daughter and best son—to the need to be best parent. Since in their self-effacing frame of reference, *best parent* is equated with *least authoritarian*, Wally fills in the gap. He has become the parent. They have become the children. There can't be two "bests." They compete. Competition is difficult for self-effacing people. They repress anger. They are confused, anxious, and unhappy. If this relationship pattern continues unchanged, Wally will become insufferably tyrannical and even antisocial.

Shirley and Frank must struggle against the need to be "good" and the need to be loved. They must establish themselves as parents and lift that responsibility from Wally. He must be given limits, and his childhood. When we get very old we sometimes become sons and daughters again and our children become our mothers and fathers. But that time has not yet arrived in the lives of this relatively young family.

People Who Move Against People

These expansive, narcissistic people view mastery as all-important. They have great need to be respected, admired, even feared. They love power. Self-assertion is of great importance to them, and aggression may be an admired quality. Friction is not avoided. They may overstate opinions and ideas and exaggerate their expertise. They usually have more experience in the real world than the other types. They abhor helplessness, respond sharply to hurt pride, and cover fear with arrogance.

Unconsciously, they often see themselves as gallant and benevolent leaders, brave, courageous, capable, powerful, and often all-knowing. They invest considerable pride in these self-idealizations, and when others contradict this self-image, their pride is hurt and they react with rage. They need people, especially as admirers, supplicants, and disciples. Their behavior to others sometimes takes on an edge of arrogant vindictiveness, the arrogance being directly proportional to their underlying fears and feelings of inadequacy. At other times they exhibit a perfectionism that can take the form of highly destructive claims on relating partners—usually claims for recognition of their helpful benevolence and respect for their strength and supposed expertise. Their partners usually see the benevolence, but often must suffer the despotism as well.

Jack, Jill, and Hazel

Jack and Hazel are married, unhappily. She can't stand "his neediness and narcissism." As she tells it:

"Nobody else in the world really exists except him. He wants admiration and homage constantly. At the same time he's a frightened crybaby who never grew up. He's a tycoon in business. Let me tell you, he ain't no tycoon in bed, or for that matter anywhere else. He is a royal *kvetch*—always worried about his health, his getting old—for Christ's sake, he's only fifty-four—his looks. Can you imagine, like a woman—he looks in the mirror a hundred times a day and is always depressed, anxious, worried—not about me or anyone else, believe me—he hasn't got the capacity to give a damn about anyone else. And because he's so completely helpless under his man-of-the-world image, he thinks all his infantile needs come first—first, last, only, and always.

"Why do I stay? Because I'm weak, too. Because it's cold out there. Because I've gotten scared over the years—and stupidly used to his lousy money—to the good life, you know—the rotten, stinking good life. Don't they say the best revenge is living well? I live well. Well in hell, but well. I hate the son-of-a-bitch—he's really a sniveling, self-centered little rat, for all his size, good looks, and money success. He fools other people, but he'd never fool any woman in his life—never."

Jill is having an affair with Jack. Hazel doesn't know about it. Of Jack, Jill says:

"I love him. I wish we had more than—what? an affair? I guess that's what it is, an affair—though to me the word doesn't begin to say what I feel. There's nothing tawdry about us and what we've got—nothing. I'm not complaining, and I thank God I've got what I've got of him. If I'd complain at all it's that I really can't do enough for him. Nothing gives me more pleasure. In sex, for instance, I like nothing better than to do anything, everything, to give him pleasure. His happiness is my happiness.

"What is he like? He's gentle, strong, warm, vital. He's a great man, I tell you, a great man. I really don't understand why he stays with that cow. He's so successful in everything else. The kids are grown up. He could get a divorce easily. But he has his reasons, his needs, and I accept that. Sometimes he's unhappy. He's like a part of me—the best part. If there was only more I could do for him—I'd do it—anything. I'm so lucky. Jack is wonderful."

Jack says:

"Why don't I leave Hazel? I really can't stand her. You ever see that French movie, *Le Chat*, with Simone Signoret and that French actor Jean Gabin? Two people who hate each other. Their hate keeps them together. They feed off it. I think it's her strength. She is strong! I like to know she's there—even though I can't stand her. And I can't stand the idea of upsetting the apple cart. And the money, too. I don't have as much as people think. But what I've got I earned. I'd have to split it with her. Not a chance—I'd never do it.

"God, that bitch is a powerhouse. So damned competent—you gotta give her that. Sex with her, though—I hate it. It's great with Jill—she's so eager to please, doesn't keep score, doesn't give a damn about herself. But I can't leave Hazel for Jill. It's been twenty-three years—I can't just throw them out the window. I've always got everything tearing me apart. I've done okay with money. But let's not kid ourselves, without my father there would have been no business. Only I know how I feel inside—how scared I feel so much of the time. Jill's a sweet thing, but let's face it, she's not a ballbreaker like Hazel; but she's not strong like her, either. If only Hazel wouldn't resent catering to me a bit."

Jack is a mixture of morbid dependency and narcissism, and the same is true of Hazel. They have most of the difficulties stemming from the admixture of two narcissists. They each make claims on the other for narcissistic supplies, and each hates the other because of this dependency. Both are chronic reminders to each other of their underlying fragility and vulnerability. Their bond, paradoxically, is strong.

Jill is a compliant, relatively dependent woman who sees Jack as strong and competent—a "man of the world," whose regard for her enhances her shaky sense of self-worth. Satisfaction through sacrifice comes easily to her, and she sees her inability to marry Jack as melodramatic material to feed a sense of self-sacrifice and devotion.

Sex with Jack is good. His aura of business success is stimulating to her; and besides, she is less interested in her response than she is in his. He responds well to her, feeling "strong and manly" in contrast to what he feels as her "soft femininity"—actually her effacing compliance. He sees his wife as harsh and masculine, though he admits she is much more beautiful than Jill.

Hazel, of course, is in a constant rage with Jack and hates sex with him mainly because he is more interested in his own pleasure than hers. She sees pleasing him as self-demeaning and as a surrender to "an uncaring infant." She further feels that despite his very good looks he is more child than man and, as such, a "turnoff." Some couples turn their antagonistic forays into a kind of foreplay, but this is not true here.

In actuality, Jack is vulnerable, fragile, and weak. Jill interprets his looks, money, business status, and narcissism as strength. Hazel suffers from the same fragility as Jack, but Jack interprets her arrogance, vindictiveness, and abrasiveness as strength. Jack and Hazel are frightened of change. They can risk nothing. They have a deep relationship, and I think they value their familial history. But they use their memories for mutual vilification as well as for morbid bonding. This is not a picture of strength by any reasonable interpretation.

Jill is much stronger than either of them. She has, in fact, the proverbial iron fist in the velvet glove. As with many outwardly self-effacing, seemingly dependent people, she is not nearly as vulnerable as people like Jack. She does not have so much shaky pride.

The fact is that Jill is able to live alone and take care of herself. When her affair with Jack is over, despite her dependency, she will survive very well. Both her flexibility and her neurosis will see her through. She will view their parting as a contribution to her sacrifice and martyrdom, which will feed her pride rather than deplete it.

People Who Move Away from People

Freedom is all-important to these detached people. They need to remain essentially uncommitted, to keep their options open, to not take sides, to remain above and distant from passionate involvement in issues and people matters. They are marked by reserve and a "mind your own business" outlook in most matters. Independence is their hallmark, and they have little difficulty sustaining an aloof attitude on most issues. They are very sensitive to coercion and abhor long-standing contracts and commitments. They do well alone but, interestingly, often need people from whom to be detached. They abhor shows of emotion, especially anger, as these may indicate excess involvement.

In their idealizations they see themselves as aloof and superior, having absolute integrity, and as being principled, strong, and silent. They hate dependency and like people to give them plenty of room.

Amanda and Raymond

It has been going on for years. They are together when they are apart, and they are apart when they are together. They live together for a few months, but they can't stand each other from the moment she or he moves in. Then they separate and promise that they will have nothing to do with each other. From the day they move apart, they pine for each other and get depressed. After a few weeks at most, they see each other once in a while and, in little more than a month, every day and night. They are "in love again." They want to be together all the time. They move in with each other. The cycle begins once again with faithful predictability.

Amanda and Raymond are both severely detached and dependent people. They suffer from equally powerful trends that cannot be satisfied at the same time. They share an inability to surrender detachment for dependency or dependency for detachment. They unconsciously attempt to satisfy both compulsions by intermittently moving together and apart.

Additionally, they have become addicted to the melodrama involved in their relationship. Each breakup and reconciliation is fraught with drama and short-lived high sexual stimulation, which masks their feelings of inner deadness. The feeling of loss and the recapture of their relationship are interpreted by them as "love."

But of late the intervals between moves have been getting shorter. The melodrama involved is losing its stimulating effect. Each has talked about the possibility of other partners. But their dependency and basic lack of self-esteem make them insecure, very possessive, and jealous. They don't want to risk losing each other; besides, they have played their game for years. Introducing additional partners may destroy what they have, and other people may not play this game as well, if at all.

So they go on moving together and apart, even though their depressions are growing more pronounced. If these depressions get very painful, perhaps they will seek help on a serious level.

Each of these character types contains aspects of other types—as we have discussed, no individual conforms *absolutely* to one mold or another, and as a result there can be great internal conflict within each individual. Many factors may intensify this sense of conflict. An insecure or emotionally difficult upbringing, marked by neglect, overprotection, or disregard for individual needs, can cause us in later life to feel anxious about our identity, forcing us into a kind of self-idealization that makes for heightened vulnerability and fragility. And our society plays a crucial role in exaggerating personality conflicts. The already *expansive*, domineering person, pushed by anxiety, becomes exploitative, arrogant, sadistic, and in some cases utterly narcissistic and self-absorbed. The *detached* person becomes seclusive, and the *self-effacing*, dependent person becomes self-effacing to the point of virtual nonexistence. Where these exaggerations take place, internal conflicts pull a person apart emotionally. He can hardly cope with himself, let alone relate to someone else in any way that even remotely resembles a fruitful level, because he projects his internal conflict onto his relating partner.

The character types we have been talking about are normal ones found among all of us. But in neurosis the various aspects of these types and the internal conflict produced by pulls in different directions become grossly exaggerated. This is also true in relating that takes place among people of similar and dissimilar types, which I will describe in the next section.

MODELS OF
RELATIONSHIPS

We can describe relationships generally by using several classifying paradigms or models. These models are not absolute—there may be some overlapping. Thus, for example, what I classify as an *antagonistic relationship* may contain at least several elements characteristic of what I would describe as a cooperative relationship. These relative models are most evident in intimate relationships, where much mutual emotional investment takes place. However, you will find that they are also applicable among business associates, friends, teachers, and students—in just about any situation in which people relate. It is valuable to remember that the dominant theme of a particular model may not be at once discernible: we may not be able to see at first the mutual *rejection* in an antagonistic relationship. But careful observation will usually give ample evidence of the identity of the model.

Cooperative Relating

The basic dynamic of a cooperative relationship is *mutual acceptance without conditions*. This means that each party to the relationship accepts the other and doesn't predicate that acceptance on conscious or unconscious conditions like these: "If you are this way"; "If you do this or that"; "As long as you give this or that."

Relating in a cooperative way is based on a crucial fact of human existence: *that the human condition, and the people representing that condition, are imperfect.* In a cooperative relationship unrealistic expectations based on mutual idealizations are minimal. Differences of opinion, discrepancies, inconsistencies in the same person, limitations of each partner, are expected and acceptable; difficulties can be understood and resolved by talking them over. They are never sources for conditional acceptance, disappointment, recrimination, and rejection.

Unconditional acceptance or acceptance without equivocation or judgment means acceptance of the total person, faults and all. It does *not* mean denial of faults or flaws in the other person, difficulties with the relationship, or self-imposed blind spots.

True unconditional acceptance is based on more than love of your relating partner. It is based on love of reality—especially of the real condition of being human, with all the assets, liabilities, and limits that being human includes and implies. This kind of love of being human can take place only in people of considerable maturity, who have observed reality well and who refuse to idealize its virtues either individually or as a general philosophy.

In a truly cooperative relationship, this basic dynamic is extended repeatedly. The partners are committed to help each other to still more understanding of reality, and themselves in the context of reality. They spend little time and energy equivocating about right and wrong; they rarely haggle over justice, reward, and punishment in the relationship; vindication ("Will you at least admit I was right all along?"), or establishing and sustaining all kinds of even balances, is of little importance to them. A couple who relate cooperatively will never have to negotiate a marriage agreement that says one party will *always* wash the dishes while the other one will *always* walk the dog. Instead, cooperative partners share with each other their problems, responsibilities, pleasures, and strong feelings about crucial priorities—especially about people. They try hard to communicate with each other. Their relationship is marked by an absence of manipulation. Messages are simple and to the point. If one partner wants to go to Saratoga Springs for the week-end, she says, "Let's go to Saratoga," not "You don't feel like staying here or going out to the Hamptons again, do you?"

And cooperative partners help each other to increase self-acceptance and self-compassion. Each *accommodates* the other—something possible only for people who are mature enough to have considerable frustration tolerance. Immature people, who must have what they want and *only what they want*, cannot accommodate or cooperate.

Cooperative partners relate as a team, but they do not attempt to merge their separate identities into one. Quite the contrary! Cooperative relating strengthens the self, because you have to use yourself in order to help your partner, and helping your partner raises your self-esteem. Cooperative partners do not make claims on each other to stimulate their caring machinery. Obviously, this kind of relationship flies in the face of our cultural values, which put a high price on self-glorification and self-satisfaction at the expense of others.

Annie and Al

He's expansive and she's compliant. He seems to rule the roost. Al decides where they will live, which vacations they'll take, how to invest money, which he budgets for them. He's decided which schools the children will attend. He is the life of the party socially. He is always buying things for the house—mainly things they have no room for and can't quite afford.

Annie goes along with Al. To some outsiders she seems to be the fragile one who "wouldn't be able to make it" without Al. They imply that he carries her as a kind of dead weight. But the same people say that Annie and Al seem very happy together, and their four children are doing very well also.

In actuality, these people have been relating on a highly co-operative basis for many years. It's true that Al is essentially expansive and Annie is essentially compliant, but this diversity of character makes it easier for them to relate constructively. And their good emotional health makes the greatest contribution to constructive relating.

These are people with a significant capacity to invest emotion, to care, to be responsible, to be open, tender, trusting, and intimate. They show these qualities to each other and to their children; the entire family enjoys the relationships they share. They like to be with one another, and a great deal of warmth, humor, feelings, and ideas are exchanged. Anger is expressed well: fights are not vindictive; grudges are not sustained. Mutual caring and welfare are prime priorities. There is considerable commonality of interests—both Annie and Al like the same books and music, the same people, feel the same way about children and about money.

If either one is indeed "stronger," it is certainly Annie. Al has more pride and is hurt more easily than Annie. As a consequence, he becomes depressed faster and for longer periods. Annie is more resilient and more flexible. She is also more realistic and practical. She "goes along," both out of compliance and because she realizes that there are a great many issues in which "it just doesn't matter that much." Unknown to most of their friends, Al discusses serious matters with Annie before decisions are made. I believe that most decisions based on sound judgment are hers, even though he makes them—or does he really? Annie returns a great many purchases that Al makes, and no one seems unhappy about that except perhaps the storekeepers.

Creative Relating

Creative relating is an extension of cooperative relating. Its principal underlying dynamic is mutual aid in the service of growth of self-realization. In this kind of relating, in addition to the characteristics of cooperative relating, each partner gives particular support to the other's creative proclivities.

Each partner functions as a kind of muse for the other. Each derives great satisfaction from his or her own as well as the other's creative self-realizing struggles and achievements. This does not mean that one partner exploits the other's supportiveness; nor does it mean that one partner lives vicariously through the other. It does mean that each partner develops an enormous sensitivity to the other's needs and aims.

In a creative relationship a unique, mutual language—verbal or nonverbal—may develop, characterized by quick and deep understanding of mutual messages. Creative partners learn to use their perceptive senses fully, as well as their total selves, as finely tuned instruments of communication. They become skilled receivers and conveyers of meaningful nuances, however subtle, especially in terms of each other's creative needs and expressions.

Mutual priorities, interests, and values aid creative relating. But the most important motivation in such a relationship is the desire to help one's partner to self-realization without personal aggrandizement as a goal. In this kind of relating there is no gray eminence; there are no background kingmakers; there are no long-suffering martyrs.

Adversary Relating

Adversary relating is the natural extension of our competitive culture and it is probably the most common kind of relationship to be found. Most people would think of it as natural and healthy; they are unaware that other possibilities exist and that adversary relating is not genetic or instinctual at root. It is an adaptation. It springs from and promotes the society with which it is consistent.

The principal underlying dynamic in adversary relating is *conditional acceptance*: one accepts one's protagonist partner *provided certain conditions are met*. These conditions usually involve the partner's helping to sustain one's own image of oneself. When, for example, one partner prides himself on his "unselfish" behavior, but becomes irritated when the other partner neglects to praise him for his self-sacrifice or his suffering, that is an adversary relationship. Each partner is preoccupied with whether the other is "being good to me" or even with me or for me. But the kind of goodness they have in mind is mostly felt in terms of their self-image, not in terms of real goodness. If one partner offers his long-suffering protagonist some help in reducing his burden of responsibilities, that will not be appreciated nearly as much as the partner's paying lip service to the other's martyrdom. The adversary contract is an unconscious, iron-bound agreement between two people to support their idealized images of themselves. Breaking the adversary contract (telling the truth) usually leads to an *antagonistic* relationship, or to termination of the relationship.

The essential ingredients of adversary relationships are competition and confrontation—almost always unconscious competition and confrontation. Indeed, adversaries often believe that they are really operating on a cooperative basis. If asked, they point to much evidence of sharing: "I do the dishes, and he buys the food." However, "sharing" in this context almost always means making sure that each partner has an equal share and that neither in any way gets ahead of the other. Balance and equality play a large role here, and "being fair" is an expression that is often used. But this concentration on equality and fairness almost always indicates an underlying need to "get ahead of," "to get more of," or a fear of "falling behind" and "being taken advantage of."

At best, these relationships are characterized by friendly jousting—not unlike "friendly competition" in doing business or the adolescent "ranking" we used to indulge in, in which the purpose was to be in a higher rank than one's friends. At their worst, adversary relationships degenerate into bickering, tantrums, or attacks of silent sulkiness—usually because one partner feels the other has not fulfilled the unspoken image-sustaining conditions that govern their relationship.

This kind of relating relies on *external* stimulation, because competition is an externalizing process. Scorekeeping, evidence-gathering, getting even, keeping lists of indiscretions and hurts, vindication, and judgmental equivocation are characteristic of adversary relating.

John and Liz

They've been married for some years now and for the most part enjoy things in common—the opera, friends, hiking, especially their children. They are both devoted to their three teenagers, whose good performance in school and obvious enjoyment of social life speak well for their family background. But John and Liz have complaints, too: John periodically feels that Liz is not supportive enough, or sufficiently appreciative of his accomplishments, which have been considerable. He says that in company she pointedly disagrees with him on issues discussed, and withholds praise when he feels it is "really appropriate." Interestingly, Liz has the same complaints. Questioning reveals that there are, in fact, stormy periods in their life, largely based on each partner feeling that the other isn't adequately supportive in terms of his/her own self-idealization.

It also becomes obvious that these people are much concerned about equal sharing of more than just mutual praise. House tasks, personal purchases, influence with the children, responsibilities toward elderly parents, uninteresting tasks of all kinds—all must be shared equally. Balance sheets are kept. There is also more than a little concern with equal sharing of sexual responsibility. These are healthy but relatively narcissistic people, engaged in a fairly typical adversary relationship of which they have virtually no conscious awareness. There is no *overt* competition between them, but it would be apparent in a business, student, or athletic-team relationship.

John and Liz have the advantage of reasonable health, much in common, and—as it happens—a fairly stable neurotic lock. He is more overtly expansive, and she is self-effacing despite underlying narcissism. Their time of greatest difficulty will probably come when their children leave home and they are thrown on their own resources to a greater degree. At that time they will make even greater claims on each other, being even more sensitive to equal billing and sharing. Their relationship will probably survive on this adversary basis, and may even increase cooperatively; but if—as sometimes happens at this stage in life—either one experiences a character change, the relationship may deteriorate into antagonism.

Antagonistic Relating

The underlying dynamic in an antagonistic relationship is *rejection*—rejection of one's partner's needs, yearnings, ideas, values, proclivities, assets, and limits, all in an attempt to block one's partner's self-realization on any level.

These partners are enemies. They consciously and unconsciously contrive methods and situations to demoralize each other and to generate hopelessness and self-hate. Each partner has an unusual need to idealize himself; when he inevitably falls short of that ideal, he experiences enormous self-hate. In actuality, each partner suffers, and is so consumed with suffering that he or she has no energy left for compassion, either for self or for the other. The relationship itself seems to consist mainly of arguments, bitterness, put-downs, and—in extreme cases—even physical assaults.

Antagonistic relating is often the end stage of a deteriorated adversary relationship. Adversary relating may go on for a lifetime, or (when the seesaw of one-upmanship in such a relationship gets unbalanced) it may deteriorate to blatant antagonism. Sudden shifts from adversary relating to antagonistic relating may be due to one partner's switching what we've called main solutions—when one partner abandons compliance for expansive narcissism. Some people, of course, never have adversary relationships at all, but go directly into being antagonists.

The hallmark of antagonistic relating is what analysts call externalization: it's always *his* or *her* fault; neither antagonist takes responsibility for what happens in the relationship. Vindictive tirades against each other and insistence on *being right* always take precedence over communication in such a relationship, and the externalizations it produces result in a kind of paradox: since each partner sees his or her hated self in the other person, they cling together in a narcissistic, self-hating frenzy and are thus morbidly close even as they pull apart.

The end results are, inevitably, increased cynicism, bitterness, hopelessness, and self-hate, as well as increased alienation from and deadening of one's own feelings.

Jim and His Bosses

Jim cannot relate to a boss except on an antagonistic level. Since his multiple bosses through the years have had no desire to relate antagonistically, each of his relationships has been short-lived, very short-lived. Jim, who is thirty-seven, has been fired from all kinds of jobs—"more than twenty times, at least."

Holding a job for Jim is crucial. He has nobody else to depend on and must have the money to live on. And, he says, "though I hate to admit it, I like to live fairly well."

Jim claims that he is an actor—"a real artist." He is not interested in "being in the business," as other would-be actors sometimes put it. He doesn't care if he "never makes a nickel out of acting." He just wants to act because it is his "form of self-expression." It is his life. In fact, he has never made any money acting. His jobs have not been related to acting in any way. He says that he would never do "commercials or any nonsense," because he would not "bastardize my craft, my art, myself." Jim has appeared in three Off Off Broadway productions (for no pay) and a number of school plays. He has taken numerous courses with various acting groups and studios. He has worked on Wall Street, in advertising, for a magazine—the list goes on and on. He has held jobs that paid from $8,000 to $34,000 a year.

Jim's "art, craft, acting," and what he thinks of as the acting world, constitute his idealized self-image. Interestingly, he subscribes to the myth that a real actor is a bohemian whose life-style precludes establishment comforts, niceties, and material needs. But Jim, as it happens, comes from a bourgeois background that he hates but that nevertheless has given him an appetite to live well. This conflict makes for great difficulty in relating to bosses at work, and in working in the mundane, bourgeois world at all. *But* he is forced to work in that world in order to live, let alone to live well.

However, his greatest difficulty in working and relating to bosses is an inability to capitulate to the work, to get in and pitch the way other people do. Indeed, he immediately reacts to authority (the boss) with rebellion, scorn, and pure hatred. Why? Because the boss and the work represent enemies to his art, to his self-idealized image, and to his imagined, idealized world. Capitulation to work means dilution of his image, bastardization of his art, and even surrender of his image.

At one point, Jim said, "I always knew I was different, and I always wanted to be different." Working like everyone else to Jim means "being the same." It means capitulation to being a crass bourgeois, which, in part, he really is, and it means activating much hate, his own, against that aspect of himself. As a consequence, Jim makes extraordinary unconscious claims on bosses. They should recognize him as the artist he is. They should give him special privileges on the job. Indeed, they ought to be patrons, forget the work and send him checks so that he can devote himself to acting.

Interestingly, despite his preoccupation with his idealization, he does very little acting. Despite all kinds of rationalizations, he acts very little because (1) his self-esteem is low, and he's actually afraid to put himself on the line; (2) he's terrified of finding out that he has no great talent, since this would result in a crumbling of his image and massive self-hate and depression; (3) he devotes more time and energy to sustaining the image of the artistic life than to the art itself; (4) fights with bosses and looking for new jobs leave little time for acting. He can thus blame bosses and an uncaring world for his own fear and inhibition in pursuing a career more actively.

Of course, he avoids doing commercials because he doesn't know if he can get them, and he is terrified by the possibility of rejection in any aspect of acting. This fear inhibits him, too, in seeking serious acting work. He is also afraid to meet other actors and the real world of acting, lest his illusions about actors and his concept of the bohemian world of acting be sullied and destroyed. He also avoids meeting "real actors" for fear he will not come off well and will not be accepted.

Obviously, what Jim needs to do is stop playing a part, stop blaming someone else's script for his problems with his life. He must come to terms with the fact that he is the author of his own script, and he must start treating his business associates as real people, not as characters in a play.

Some overlapping among models of relationships takes place— there may be antagonistic moments between even the healthiest cooperative partners. But for the most part the major mode of a relating couple remains essentially constant. This means that, if we look for the underlying dynamic, it will tell us how these people relate, in most instances, with remarkable fidelity.

Changing from antagonistic to adversary relating entails much struggle, and from antagonistic to cooperative relating, a struggle of heroic proportions. To go from adversary to cooperative relating, let alone to creative relating, is possible, but this requires enormous motivation—almost always lacking—and usually long and profound psychoanalysis. Changing in a healthy direction, however fruitful the consequences, is invariably fraught with difficulty and resistance, of which the analyst is only too aware. People cling to the familiar, even when the familiar is horrendous, painful, stultifying, and destructive. Moving into unfamiliar territory, however uplifting it may be, usually initiates considerable anxiety. Simply put, we tend to be afraid of the unknown, and a step in the direction of cooperative relating always entails at least some trust of ourselves and our partners. But this step is mandatory if we are to derive the real satisfaction only to be found by tapping our own resources in the service of cooperative relationships.

II

NEUROTIC
LOCKS

NEUROTIC LOCKS

When people are compulsively bound together by neurotic needs (usually unconscious) instead of being linked by free choice and conscious decision, I say they are victims of *neurotic lock*. The lock is most powerful where the individuals involved are least healthy, least in touch with their feelings; such a bond is extremely painful to break. In fact, some locks are never broken; some *are* broken, only to be re-created with other partners.

Now, how does this almost organic bonding derive its strength—where does the attracting and binding emotional glue come from? Karen Horney's concept of character structure, some of which I described earlier, is especially pertinent here. Remember the three general character types she described—self-effacing, expansive, and detached—and remember that in almost all of us, one of these trends, which Horney calls the principal or main solution, is most dominant, identified with, and used in conscious relating to people. The others are submerged or repressed out of conscious awareness, so as to prevent conflict in feelings, goals, and behavior. Thus, the expansive-narcissistic or expansive-aggressive, perfectionistic person will hide his or her self-effacing dependency trend and his detached trend from himself and others. A detached, non-involved, independence-loving person will hide his/her dependency and expansive trends, and a self-effacing person will hide his/her expansive and detached trends.

But the submerged trends do not go away. They require sustenance, too. They are part of our unconscious idealized image of ourselves; they help to form the system of "shoulds" that tell us what we can and can't do in order to maintain this idealized image. When we behave in a way that contradicts one "should" image—when someone who sees himself as an unselfish (compliant) person suddenly acts in response to his repressed aggressive (or expansive) impulses—this contradiction can bring on punishing attacks of self-hatred that make any relationship painful.

Yet denying those repressed trends can be just as painful. Unconsciously, we attempt to see ourselves as (expansive) strong, all-knowing, and masterful, even as we see ourselves as (self-effacing) utterly lovable, fragile, loyal, more concerned about others than self, even as we see ourselves as (detached) aloof, reserved, independent of need of people, and free of any obligating involvements. But, as I said, it is impossible to sustain this image of conflicting trends and needs. We are each of us composed of myriad conflicting characteristics, and no psychological stratagem can result in an even near-perfect integration of the various aspects of ourselves. But we try—and we also try to feed each of our needs, healthy ones as well as those whose intensity and compelling requirements have reached neurotic proportion. Without conscious awareness, but with powerful force and motivation, we seek and are attracted to persons who can satisfy our need to *nourish* our hidden trends. Another way to put this is to say that we seek an idealized partner, but the idealization is a projection of those aspects of ourselves that we usually hide from ourselves. *The satisfaction of the hidden trend through vicarious identification with the other person is what freezes the lock.*

Thus, the ideal *lock position* would be between people who have much in common—cultural background and frame of reference, sexual attraction (largely determined by early training, subculture, and experience)—but who have different main characterological trends. They have enough in common to bring them together, and each one acts out the character trend that the other represses. Occasionally, largely due to sexual attraction and lack of knowledge of each other, people of the same trend form close relationships. Mutual dissatisfaction ensues unless they are very healthy and liberated from the power of these unconscious and compelling trends and needs. This misadventure happens most commonly in narcissistic people who sometimes are attracted to mirror images of themselves for obvious reasons.

Paradoxically, people whose character goals are different (e.g., expansive people who move against people and self-effacing people who move toward people and/or detached people who move away from people) get along together even as they complain of differences, because their differences satisfy their hidden trends and needs.

If people switch main trends through analysis, maturation, or trauma (like the couple on pages 111–113), they may have much more in common consciously, but neither one will satisfy the unconscious needs of the other and the relationship may run into difficulty. The "switch" acts as an effective emotional solvent—but not necessarily a healthy one. Often this difficulty is initially described as boredom with each other. Often other relationships are sought in an effort to satisfy unconscious trend needs vicariously. Unless these needs are exposed, diluted, and diminished in their intensity, it is almost impossible to transform the relationship from destructive to constructive.

Now let us examine some of the possibilities in the various mixes of character trends. We will assume that these are largely neurotic for two reasons. First, because most of us relate neurotically in large degree, and second, because once we understand exaggerated versions it will be easier to apply that understanding to more subtle versions of the same manifestations.

Self-effacing/Expansive

The self-effacing person wants, more than anything, a relationship in which he or she can be identified with strength, know-how, and direction; he is looking for the perfect partner to depend on. He *me* feels that love will bind them together and will provide an adequate self to replace the one that has been effaced. He equates forceful-ness with strong potential for love.

The expansive person is attracted by his or her partner's need for love and translates this need by seeing a person who can be *Damien* directed, taken care of, and above all counted on for floods of ad-miration. This person gives him the chance to exercise his benev-olent despotism. When perfectionism and arrogant vindictiveness are also present in high degree, and they often are in narcissists, self-effacing people provide the best outlets.

Though he may not admit it, the extreme expansive narcissist really feels he owns everybody and everything in his household. He may not consult his partner on major decisions because she is, after all, only an extension of himself. Does he consult his right hand? Of course not. He simply expects it to do his bidding and to comply with decisions made by him.

On an unconscious level the expansive person lives out his dependency needs through his overtly dependent partner. The self-effacing partner lives out aggressive needs through an overtly ex-pansive partner.

All other considerations being equal, these partners get along well. Considerable cooperation may be in evidence, because their character trends are complementary. If these character trends are not too intense, and if nothing upsets the unspoken and uncon-scious agreements governing the relationship, they may cooperate forever. But if they are neurotic enough, expansive and self-effacing individuals form very strong locks. They are essentially people-oriented rather than principle-oriented: loyalty is a greater priority for them than integrity. Since both of them require loyalty, though each would interpret the word differently, they get along well—a fair exchange is no robbery. In extreme cases they are capable of sadomasochistic relating: the expansive person can be vindictive, often through open, verbal castigation, while the self-effacing person is an expert at generating and sustaining painful guilt in a partner. In addition, the self-effacing person usually has a highly developed detached streak and knows very well how to create pain by cutting off and ignoring a needy partner.

Most difficulties between these partners arise when expectations, both conscious and unconscious, are unfulfilled and claims are thwarted, which especially occurs in changes of principal solutions. Thus, the expansive person is disappointed when his dependent partner suddenly denies him admiration and blind obedience. Self-assertion is interpreted as disloyalty, because it means that the self-effacing partner will no longer allow the expansive one to live out his own dependency needs. And the expansive partner's own dependency trend may begin to surface if it is not hidden by his subjugation of his partner and lived out through that partner. This threat may create enough anxiety to force him to seek a new disciple.

Self-effacing people are disappointed if they are not treated as loving, martyred, self-sacrificing, saintly people, and if they don't receive loving care. They cannot tolerate having their claims thwarted—especially those based on love: "If you love me, you would rather be with me than at work." They are upset unconsciously when the expansive person demonstrates "weakness," because such behavior deprives the dependent partner of a crutch, of a self to subjugate oneself to, of meaningful love (which is felt as meaningful only if it comes from a so-called strong person), and of direction. To be called on to fall back on one's own resources is very frightening to a person who believes he or she has none. If the partner suddenly becomes dependent, the self-effacing person's own expansive trend may surface and throw him or her into deep conflict and chaos. He or she may choose to seek a "stronger" partner, or accept a role reversal, or struggle for extrication from the relationship and assertion of his or her real self.

It should be pointed out that in highly neurotic people, especially those in this particular neurotic lock, much mutual dependency is ever present. This means that each depends on the other for a personal sense of identification, be it through seeming active mastery or passive dependency. In short, each functions as a kind of emotional crutch for the other. Even though we use a crutch, we don't like it because it reminds us of our infirmity. Therefore, it is common for people in this lock to repress much anger at each other, anger that comes from resentment of personal dependency. Any thwarted claim—such as the statement "If you love me, you'd agree with me" or "If you love me, you'd stay with me"—is likely to tap the pool of anger, which may then bring on a seemingly inappropriate response. It is easier for the expansive partner to express anger, but although self-effacing people are afraid of anger, they are also capable of duplicitous expression through subtle forms of sabotage. Also, when self-effacing people sense an expansive partner weakening, as in a momentary period of hurt pride and loss of synthetic self-esteem, they often spring to the attack—although they will usually retreat when the expansive partner reestablishes his or her former position. Some people, once they taste power and emergence from thralldom, cannot retreat, and this may signal either a long struggle for healthier relating, a shift of neurotic power, or termination of the relationship. But usually, people quickly reform the status quo and continue in the neurotic lock. Healthy unlocking requires conscious exposure of the "shoulds" of personal conflicting trends and realization of how one has exploited one's partner to satisfy those trends.

Molly and Paul

Molly is Paul's mother. She is an old woman now, and he is a middle-aged man. Molly's husband, Dan, Paul's father, died ten years ago. Since Dan's death, a great change has taken place in this mother/son relationship. They used to get along very well, and there was much mutual devotion between them.

Molly was always a homebody, self-effacing, seemingly dependent. Her life was dedicated to being "a wife, a mother, a homemaker." Dan was expansive, protective of his family, and quite directive with both his wife and his son. Paul married early, had children early, was expansive like his father, and became fairly successful in business. He too is devoted to his family, but also tends to be despotic, in a benevolent way.

Up to the time of her husband's death, Paul was the apple of Molly's eye. He could do no wrong. She felt very close to him and on rare occasions complained of Dan's despotism to him.

After Dan's death, Molly became chronically depressed. Her conversation was full of self-derisive remarks. She said that her life had been wasted, and periodically repeated that she had been a fool not to have stood up to Dan and told him that she "was a person, too" and that it was "too late now." She also repeated that "without him I'm a nothing and a nobody."

Since Dan's death, Molly has become increasingly hostile to Paul and to his family, whom she always adored. She sometimes denies her anger, but obviously finds it impossible to keep from "saying things that are awful, and then I want to bite my tongue." At various times Paul and his family have stayed away from her. He feels hurt and rejected—"rejected without justification"—and he also feels that his presence only exacerbates her condition.

One obvious way she attempts to curtail her anger is to become more self-effacing, more of a martyr than ever. But this does not help her; in fact, it irritates anyone who is in her presence. She makes remarks like "I should have died instead of your father" or "Perhaps I won't wake up tomorrow, and that will relieve you of your burden"; unconsciously, she is trying (at least in part) to generate guilt, and such forms of hostility are not lost on those to whom they are directed. Paul and his wife dread seeing his mother or even talking to her on the phone. They "wish she was the way she used to be."

There is little that is subtle or difficult to figure out here. Molly was abandoned by Dan, the strong oak on whom she was a clinging vine. This abandonment—or rejection—has generated rage, which in turn has ignited a whole storehouse of repressed hostility. The abandonment has deprived Molly of a self (she had merged her identity with Dan's in an interdependency lock) and also of any hope of venting her anger at him in the future. Molly and Dan represented a strong self-effacing/expansive lock. In view of her age and her continued devotion to her dead husband, there was little chance for Molly to re-create the lock with someone else when her partner abandoned her. It was also too late and too frightening to shift gears—to become expansive consciously. She felt like a "nobody," but nevertheless a nobody with uncontrollable anger.

She did what was safe and convenient. She displaced her feelings of hostility—repressed until now—from Dan to her son, Paul. This, of course, was made easier by Paul's identification with his father (they were both expansive). In expressing her hostility, expansive vindictive aspects of Molly's personality, formerly repressed, came to the fore. She could trust her son more than her husband, and now she allowed herself to experience, rather than deny, her real feelings. This probably had a therapeutic effect on Molly. Of course, Paul was confused by the change in his mother, as would his father have been if the change had taken place while he was alive. However, this change was not complete. Molly continued to be self-effacing, martyred, guilt-producing to all concerned, but she continued to be hostile to Paul at the same time—having found a way to straddle the fence. Almost the best she and Paul can hope for is a kind of benign adversary relationship: she will accept him on certain conditions, conditions she would have preferred to have imposed on her late husband, Dan.

Self-effacing/Self-effacing

These pairs are often frightened people who relate to each other largely because they are afraid of other possibilities. They are attracted by the fact that neither appears threateningly assertive to the other.

Sometimes, however, these combinations are the result of "mistakes," in which a momentary episode of expansiveness was viewed as the real thing but soon turned out to be self-effacement after all—such as when a shy man turns out, paradoxically, to be a "strong" dancer and frightens off a compliant partner. In any case, these people are often overwhelmed by an explosion of mutual acceptance, since acceptance and exchange of love are so important to them.

They are both people-oriented, loyalty-oriented, and may also have much else in common. They may have the same social aspirations, to be liked and thought of as nice people.

But self-effacing people do not have the worldliness found in masterful, expansive narcissists. Also, they offer each other no possibility of vicarious identification with overt expansiveness. Claims made on each other for direction and leadership go unheeded. They become a classic case of "After you, Alphonse," "After you, Gaston"—the old joke about the two Frenchmen who refuse to be the first to go through the door—neither being willing to take the initiative or to offer direction or make decisions. Both suppress their desire to please the other; thus, neither is pleased and both are angry. But since anger is difficult for them to express, it is bottled up, which usually leads to further complications, including depression and even physical complaints (stomach upsets, respiratory difficulties, migraines, and so on). These are often used as a basis for martyrdom or claims for special treatment, as the two self-effacing partners compete to see which one is the more miserable.

Unlike expansive narcissists, these people are not self-igniting and tend to secretly envy people who seem to enjoy spicier, more interesting lives.

The self-effacing/self-effacing lock is fairly common in friendships, where a group of people can sit around all evening discussing what to eat, where to go, without anyone being willing to make a decision, and in business, where we see it operate in decision making by committee.

Couples finding themselves in this lock are liable to suffer from inertia and inability to tap inner resources on their own behalf.

Sometimes they suffer from mild to moderate chronic depression and feel that other people are either more talented or luckier than they are. Their condition does not preclude claims on each other, especially for still more love and understanding, still more evidence of caring, and for decisions and directions. These not being forth-coming from an equally self-effacing partner, the pair may find themselves locked in repressed hostility, confusion, and still more stagnation. They will have reached a stalemate resulting from the failed claim each has made on the other.

With insight, these people are capable of considerable sensi-tivity to each other's dilemma—and sometimes a good deal of com-passion, too. They may even struggle to help themselves and each other to greater self-assertion. But without insight they cannot sat-isfy each other's needs, either consciously or unconsciously, and so the relationship is doomed to frustration.

Breaking up is difficult, because neither of the self-effacing partners is expansive or aggressive enough to make the move. Also, these people tend to form extremely strong, morbid dependent bonds, since dependency is a major dynamic and a well-practiced one in their lives. Should the death of one partner occur, however, there is a tendency to seek out a really expansive person next time around.

Detached/Detached

Why do detached people form relationships at all? My analyst, Nat Freeman, used to say detached people need people to be detached from. Actually, detached people back into relationships, and the attraction of *another* detached person is usually lack of threat as well as commonality. They are both, after all, principle- and integrity-oriented rather than people- and loyalty-oriented.

These are people whom Karen Horney describes as being "exquisitely sensitive" to coercion—people to whom freedom is of paramount importance. They are extremely wary of "heavy in-volvements" and tend to back into situations rather than to go forward into them. The latter would indicate too much interest, too much involvement, and too much contact. But underneath all their aloofness they follow other personality trends, too. They do need people. They make mistakes, and when they misread their partners, they live like ships that pass in the night, often leading separate lives together.

Much depends on the intensity of the compulsion toward detachment. Loyalty does not bind these people, but integrity does— it is a principle. This means that if staying together represents the "right" thing, they may stick, because the investment of pride in integrity and principle is powerful even if it isn't personal. On a conscious level they may have relatively few complaints. But *unconscious* yearnings for expansive mastery and compliant dependency and "love" may be unrequited, and so each partner may feel considerable disquietude. This is usually experienced as anxiety.

Such people rarely indulge in fights or sadomasochistic activity, because these would represent too much involvement and commitment. Keeping one's distance is, after all, very important here. If one of the partners attempts to move closer (if, for example, he or she wants to try another way of relating), the other will move away (or maybe even out). Moving away can create a tango effect: partner number 1 moves still closer; partner number 2 retreats another step. Since neither can satisfy the repressed needs of the other through behavior, the couple may drift apart. I do not use the word *drift* here whimsically. Leaving each other or breaking up would require too much emotional effort and go against the dictum of noninvestment and noncommitment in issues. If the relationship is over, it usually dissolves by attrition; but often it will continue, largely through inertia. It is valuable to remember that it is always easier for people with pride in independence to let go, and detached people see themselves as independent above all; though they may never take steps to break up a relationship, they may simply back out of it by lack of input.

Laura and Jeremy

Laura says, "Our difficulties started when we got married. No; when I look back, I realize they started even earlier, as soon as we decided to get married. Until then it was okay, more than okay. It was good, very good, and after that it's been all downhill."

Jeremy continues, "Laura's right. Though even before that I remember her telling me she had a funny dream. Seems in the dream she couldn't stand the fact that if we ever got married we'd both be using the same bathroom the rest of our lives."

Laura says, "Before the wedding—I mean about a week before—I felt very queasy. But Jeremy was worse. He went into a complete funk, a real panic—couldn't eat, couldn't sleep—nearly called the whole thing off."

And Jeremy rejoins, "We were doing all right. Had our own jobs. Saw each other a lot. Stayed out of each other's way. I still don't know why we did it. She wasn't that anxious. I think it was our families. Mostly hers. After we moved in together, we still did okay. Now it's like we're always in each other's way."

Laura is giggling now. "Maybe we should get separate apartments. Everything just seems heavy. Sex too—like a chore."

Jeremy isn't amused. "It's not so funny. That's when we were happiest. Sex was best then, too."

Questioning and discussion revealed to me that these were two very detached people with extreme sensitivity to coercion. Privacy played an enormous role in their lives. Despite their sensitivity to coercion, they married as a result of family pressure and the need to conform to cultural standards—each of them had a strong underlying trend of compliancy. Commitment was the straw that broke the camel's back, but there already was a considerable load under that straw. They had been very detached people all their lives and had always functioned at a considerable emotional distance from other people.

They had a "neat arrangement" before they decided on marriage; in fact, they had separate apartments, lived their lives on an individual basis, and saw each other fairly often, sometimes staying over at each other's house (on invitation) for weekends. They felt happy.

Commitment made them feel trapped, as if they were giving up something very important. Further questioning revealed considerable externalization, too. Each accused the other of insensitivity to individual needs and standards. Moving in together (prior to commitment) was traumatic and turbulent but manageable, but once they had committed themselves to marriage, they admitted, they both began to miss living in separate quarters. It turned out that Laura's dream and dread of sharing a single bathroom occurred the night they decided to get married.

The marriage ceremony—a public act witnessed by friends—and the legal status it brought accelerated the decline of their former happiness. Jeremy admitted that his panic was so great just prior to the ceremony that he thought he would "run away and get lost." He said he knew "how it felt to be sold into slavery." Laura said she felt very sad—"like something very heavy was about to happen. I was supposed to be sad, and here I was, sad." She made an interesting slip here, using the word *sad* instead of *glad*.

Although I suggested therapy for each of them before making any move at all, they said they would think it over—therapy is, after all, a considerable commitment, too. On the way out, Jeremy laughingly said that if they didn't care what people thought, maybe they'd get divorced and go back to their old, happy way of life. My own thought was that detached people are capable of a great deal of resignation—despite their unhappiness, Jeremy and Laura might go on this way indefinitely, especially if their underlying dependency, compliancy, and conformity trends are strong.

Expansive Narcissist/Expansive Narcissist

If people of the same persuasion form a relationship, it is most likely to occur between narcissists. These people are often "doers." They need admiration, an audience—so they need to have much to do with other people. They don't wait for an audience to come to them or for their wishes to be magically granted: they *do* something about it; they act. At times the act creates situations they did not count on at all. These people are highly vulnerable to "pride tickles"—anything that stimulates their pride or has the potential to satisfy pride needs. So they are easily *attracted* to each other because they often take pains to *be attractive*. Often this attraction turns out to be a case of love at first sight (mirror images are easy to become infatuated with if one has always been infatuated with one's self) and hate ever after.

Of course, expansive people have many common interests, and this draws them together. They are people- and loyalty-oriented and are not hemmed in by either principle or a great investment in integrity. They think big, are gregarious, like nice things, have energy, like to be with people, especially those who give them loyalty and admiration. They like position and power. They usually learn to cope in the world, however junglelike it turns out to be.

Expansive narcissist couples are often seen in the show-business world, but they are common elsewhere as well. They are frequently admired, as couples, by people who don't really know them and who see them as worldly, talented, capable, and fun-loving. They may also be seen as opportunistic, pushy, and domineering, self-centered, given to exaggeration and embellishment, and sometimes shallow and superficial. This kind of a relationship *can* run smoothly: the very fact that both partners are working in tandem, with the common goal of ample admiration for the team, helps keep them together.

But even this kind of teamwork has its pitfalls. The fact is that neither partner provides the other with exclusive rights to narcissistic supplies—admiration, approval, acclaim—and there is seldom enough to go around. It is also virtually impossible for either partner to serve two masters—especially when, as in this case, both masters want complete mastery. These people usually have strong preferences, tastes, opinions, and ideas about rights and wrongs. They are usually perfectionistic and have a considerable capacity for arrogant vindictiveness. In addition, they equate anger and its expression with strength. When the other partner is not accommodating enough, or does not measure up to standards, fights between them may be inevitable, and also monumental and destructive.

This kind of relationship can take on sadomasochistic overtones intermittently, but a real sadomasochistic lock (see pages 81–84) cannot really be established, since neither partner is inclined to take on the role of masochist. But it is easy to hurt the narcissist, whose pride in mastery and need for admiration are always in jeopardy; when that pride and need are frustrated, the narcissist's underlying self-effacement surfaces, turning him/her into a temporary masochist until pride is restored through new victories or rationalized retreats.

The real problem with an expansive/expansive lock is that neither partner offers the other any vehicle for expressing unconscious self-effacement and detachment. These people hate—and repress—their own self-effacement and detachment; so they have contempt for people who are openly self-effacing and they lack understanding for openly detached people. Yet they hate each other for not providing vehicles to live out the hated trends they themselves repress. Perversely, they also hate the other partner for not playing the role of willing disciple 100 percent, so that *they* can play the role of benevolent despot.

As I've said earlier, expansive narcissists provide quite a show for other people, but they are often hell for each other. Unless these couples are relatively healthy, unless their character trends—overt and repressed—are essentially lacking in intensity and compulsivity, they usually break up gratefully and seek people of other character solutions.

On occasion some of these people experience enough hurt pride to suffer severe attacks of depression, as a result of which they seek therapy. Successful treatment reveals the expansive trend to be largely a reaction to a basic lack of self-esteem and a *fear* of self-effacement. This revelation makes relating easier: if *both* partners are motivated to seek help, this kind of relationship can become constructive rather than destructive.

Bill and Joe

They were both successful businessmen, were well acquainted, though not great friends, and decided to go into business together. At first the business flourished, as did their friendship—or so it seemed. In fact, they couldn't see enough of each other; so much so that their wives (both self-effacing people) objected to the necessity of having to include the other in every social situation. But after several months subtle changes began to take place. First, there were small irritations. Then, there was much discussion about who would be in charge of what. As time passed, accusations began. Bill said that Joe was undermining Bill's authority in the company, and vice versa. It soon became apparent that they were vying with each other for admiration and declarations of undiluted loyalty from fellow executives in the company and from any employee with whom they came into contact.

Initially they didn't seem to care at all about who would be president and who would be vice-president of the company. However, within a year of the formation of the partnership, this question became an acrimonious issue that seemed to have no solution. Finally, the company was forced to form a meaningless board, so that one could be chairman and one president; it was decided that these roles would be switched intermittently. But even this did not help. They both became increasingly paranoid, each accusing the other of manipulations involving employees, clients, and finally money, too. Actually, they were both honest men, but they were caught in what had become an antagonistic relationship. Both were terrified that the other would usurp both mastery and narcissistic supplies. Within eighteen months the company was dissolved, to the detriment of both men. Needless to say, their joint social life had deteriorated months earlier. Interestingly, their wives wanted to continue to see each other; but the husbands saw this as profound disloyalty, and their self-effacing wives complied.

By the completion of the breakup of the business, each man had a long list of indiscretions, inadequacies, and "crimes" committed by the other; in actuality, they were both capable, talented businessmen who had formed an impossible neurotic lock that had started out on a cooperative basis but deteriorated into malignant antagonism. They were convinced they would always be enemies, and both of them harbored paranoid fantasies of what the other might do to "get even."

Detached/Expansive

The attraction between detached people and expansive ones is largely that of seeming opposites. When something is going badly, the expansive person wants to change it or to conquer it, the detached person wants to ignore it. When something has been "good" (sex, food, etc.), the expansive person wants more of it, the detached person has had enough of it—and so it goes. The expansive person is attracted to the detached person's reserve, silence, integrity, attention to and investment in principle, independence, coolness, and self-control—which are seen as craftiness, intelligence, hidden abilities of all kinds, strength, or wisdom. These attributes are very attractive to a person whose own quest for admiration makes him or her feel a constant vulnerability covered up by manipulation of truths. Silence is attractive to a person who values mastery but who cannot keep quiet. They are sure that the detached person has all kinds of hidden wisdom, as well as self-control, which has great appeal to people who worship control in any form. The detached person also offers relatively little resistance to the narcissist's moves and demands as long as they do not become too coercive or attack personal integrity. The expansive person interprets this lack of resistance as the behavior of a compliant disciple—and a lock is forged.

Actually, it is a fairly tenable lock. Each partner offers the other some attractive options. But eventually strains and cracks appear.

The detached person's insistence on truth above all, at best, only gets in the way of the expansive person's exaggerations and manipulations. It may also make the narcissist feel like a liar by comparison. The expansive person may start expounding his critical theories about the ballet, and the detached partner may interrupt, reminding the expansive one that he's seen only two ballets in his life and walked out on both of them. At worst, if the detached person levels accusations of truth-tampering, altering the narcissist's own picture of himself or herself, this may be interpreted as disloyalty.

Eventually it will become increasingly difficult for the expansive person to manipulate the detached partner, or even to manipulate other people in the presence of the detached partner. What started out as unassertive detachment becomes a stubborn surveillance.

Additionally, the detached person is not people-oriented. He/she is loyal to principle. The two partners will therefore have different needs and appetites and ideas about—for instance—their social life. If they are a couple, the expansive person may feel that they live like hermits, while the detached partner feels they are inundated by a constant stream of people they don't really care to be with. A typical fight between an expansive and a detached partner might erupt over the former's twisting the truth in order to help a friend—something that the detached person will not, and indeed cannot, do. Pride invested in truth does not permit this assault on one's image of integrity.

Eventually the expansive partner may come to feel that he/she is dragging a huge whale over dry land: all his/her ideas and enthusiasms are dampened and deadened by an unenthusiastic, inhibiting party-pooper who always seems to see the reasonable, logical side of issues and decisions rather than the promising, glittery, fun side. The expansive person experiences the detached person's need for privacy as rejection and disloyalty, and this is painful indeed. And when, in an effort to make contact, the expansive partner tries to start a fight, the detached partner often just withdraws and closes up—a powerful punishment to expansive people.

On an unconscious level the detached partner gives the expansive person a chance to live through some of his/her detachment and need for quietness, integrity, and independence. But a detached person offers almost no opportunity for the expansive partner to vicariously identify with his own repressed, self-effacing trend: detached people are usually *not* overtly compliant, no matter how unassertive they may seem to be.

The detached person makes a poor disciple on a conscious level, but interestingly offers the expansive person a chance to act out his compliancy consciously. What I mean is, the expansive person acts out his compliancy at the shrine of his partner's integrity. He may idolize his partner's indifference to people's opinions, likes and dislikes, and admiration. This relating pair is the one combination in which the expansive person may often become a disciple and supplicant. He often resents this position, and it generates self-hate and vindictive tirades, but it has a binding effect nevertheless.

The detached person may be attracted and repelled at the same time by the expansive one. The narcissistic partner's bombast is not easy to take, nor are the obvious maneuvers for admiration and support, nor the constant use of superlatives or the exaggerations and bending of truths. But stimulation is very attractive to someone with the detached person's resigned temperament, and the expansive person is often stimulating. Expansive people seem to offer vitality and a chance to experience expansiveness vicariously. And if the detached person has repressed his own expansive tendencies, he is unconsciously gratified by the way the expansive person puts him in the position of superior partner, looking up to him as a center of wisdom and solidity. In this way the detached person also lives out some of his/her self-effacement through the expansive partner's self-effacing approach to his/her detached partner. This undoubtedly seems rather convoluted, but it must be remembered that the human condition and the unconscious are extremely complex.

If the expansive person feels as if he's dragging a whale over dry land, the detached person often feels she has a tiger with a toothache by the tail: coerced, put upon, inundated, invaded, stripped of privacy.

The expansive partner feels that his/her partner withholds, never enters fully into the relationship, is cold, ungiving, and too independent. "I want to share a few lines I'm reading aloud to her and she resents it." The expansive partner feels that the detached person is terribly stingy with praise and admiration. The detached partner feels his/her partner is "a loud-mouthed, abrasive buffoon, a lovable screwball, an interfering nuisance who never leaves me alone." Says the detached partner, "I can't sit quietly for a while with my own thoughts without his interrupting me about something or other."

One likes to—needs to—socialize. The other doesn't, preferring to be with people at fewer times, in fewer numbers. One goes overboard in her enthusiasms for people; the other is reserved and waits until he makes a judgment or invests in a relationship. The detached person plans ahead; the expansive person wants to do it now!

Despite complaints, these people are capable of a very strong bond. One provides caution, truth, and stability; the other provides an escape from inertia, movement, and excitement. When they break up, it is often because the severely detached, resigned partner feels that he/she is "drowning" in the relationship and losing her/his sense of identity. The severely expansive narcissist feels that he/she is living with a person who is "dead," who "gives nothing," and who as a result suffers from a critical shortage of narcissistic supplies. The detached person is the least likely of all types to give flattery, however much it may smooth the way, because it is contrary to the rule of integrity and principle above all.

Fanny, Benny, and Pam

I call this story a case of mistaken identity.

I never met Benny and Pam. I only know about them through Fanny.

Fanny had been suffering from severe anxiety and moderate depression for about six years, although she had no idea why she was anxious or unhappy, and she had virtually no insight about herself generally. Of late her anxiety had taken the form of panic attacks in which she felt so disorganized and disoriented that she literally did not know what to do next. She was very frightened and felt that she might have to give up a successful professional career and "just stay at home." Benny, her husband for the last nine years, did everything she asked, but nothing helped. Pam, whom she dearly loved, cheered her a bit—but even Pam's company did not dispel the nameless panic that gripped her. Pam was a small Siamese cat; they had had her for seven years.

Fanny described her early background as a very impoverished one. She was the youngest of three sisters, and her family could never afford anything more than a three-room apartment in a rather run-down neighborhood. Her mother was an "unhappy, angry, envious" woman who despised her truck-driver husband and taught her girls that he was "stupid, inept, and someone to have only contempt for." Fanny's mother blamed their life of poverty on what she called a barely literate man and a very bad marriage. Fanny, in turn, describes her father as "a nonentity" who complied with everything everyone wanted; she never heard him complain about anything, and despite "being treated like a dog in the house," he seemed "stupidly content."

Fanny's mother displaced much rage and contempt on to her daughters. Fanny cannot remember a "single word of praise or encouragement ever." Her mother often told Fanny that she was ugly—and stupid like her father. Neither was at all true. But Fanny believed her, and "as a result I never dreamed of going to college. Besides, my mother taught us that money was everything." Fanny felt herself worthless, and soon formed the belief that only marriage to a successful, rich man could save her from misery.

The only (indirect) praise she ever got from her mother was the suggestion that *she could* and must marry a real man—*real* being the antithesis of her father—above all a *rich* man. The stress her mother placed on money was enormous, and from an early age

Fanny began to have vindictive, triumphant fantasies involving money. These fantasies became almost her only source of relief from feelings of abuse and were directly proportional to her feelings of impoverishment. Eventually the idea of having a million dollars was not enough. She thought in terms of hundreds of millions. Even when she was earning several hundred thousand dollars a year, she still felt like "a poor person."

The road to this kind of money was obvious. It could not be through her own skills as an earner. It would be through a man—a man who would be the antithesis of her own father, whom she saw as a continued source of embarrassment.

During her formative years Fanny became an addict of movie magazines. She was convinced that movie stars, having both money and celebrity status, lived in a kind of heaven on earth removed from and defended against the limitations and difficulties encountered by plain people.

And then she met Benny. She knew as soon as she saw him: "It was love at first sight." Benny was, she thought, everything her father wasn't. Benny would be her savior. He was good-looking, like some of her movie idols. More important, he earned $40,000 a year as a business executive and "seemed to be really going places." This was at a time when men earned $10,000 or $12,000 a year and $20,000 was considered a superb income. At that point in time Fanny earned $7,000 a year. They married. There was initial passion, "for about six weeks," and then everything quieted down. Fanny changed jobs. They bought a Siamese cat and named her Pam.

Fanny made more and more money. Benny didn't. Fanny became her company's star producer. Benny didn't. Before too long Fanny was earning four times what Benny did. Pam purred, and Benny and Fanny loved her. Benny was content. But Fanny was not, and somewhere along the line she began to have anxiety attacks—actually they correlated with each of her new business victories, which became more common. Benny and Pam remained content and indifferent.

Fanny was increasingly aware of grievous disappointment with

Benny and frustration at her inability to move him beyond the position he had attained. But she repressed these feelings of anger. Their sex life was almost nil. Occasional contact took place, always initiated by Fanny. She thought of leaving Benny, but she couldn't. He was always nice to her, particularly when she was depressed—and when she was depressed, which was more and more frequent, she needed him especially. But when she wasn't depressed, she had contempt for the way in which he did everything for her and their small household. His solicitousness was then interpreted as non-manly weakness.

Fanny realized that she had somehow married a man just like her father. Benny was the opposite of what she had thought. He was not "a big shot after all." He would never be rich or famous or anything like the movie people she had read about as a child. She had fooled herself. It was a case of mistaken identity.

Benny was firmly entrenched in his position of detached resignation and had no intention of budging. He told Fanny many times that he was happy with his job, wanted no promotions or further headaches. He meant it, and when she pressured him and threatened to leave, he said she could if she had to, but he would in no way change; he knew that he was okay and needed no help at all. He continued to help her in any way that did not involve personal change, especially when she was depressed or anxious. He shopped, cleaned, cooked, took care of Pam (who didn't need much care, Siamese cats being very independent).

Fanny was trapped. Her strong underlying dependency needs made the contemplation of being alone very frightening, especially when she was depressed or having anxiety attacks. Besides, Benny was "really a wonderful guy" who never gave her a hard time and was always there to lean on. But she hated herself for being married to a prototype of her father after all. She was embarrassed by Benny's lowly status. She dreaded going to company parties with him and suffered from severe anxiety each time a social meeting with "big shots, real big shots" came up. But her expansive trend was strong, and despite her misery, her business ability continued to grow; she made more and more money, widening the gap between Benny's income and her own, and increasing her contempt for him and herself.

Fanny is a very expansive but dependent woman of minimal real self-esteem who has married a prototype of her father. She may have been duped by what seemed to her Benny's lofty position when they met; she may also have been unconsciously attracted to her father and displaced some of these feelings to Benny in an attempt to resolve unfinished childhood yearnings.

Initially she formed both a dependent and a competitive relationship with this man, eventually no longer needing him to compete with her but continuing to be dependent. Dependency prevented her from leaving, but it made her feel rage at being entrapped. And yet she had to repress this anger, because expressing it would have upset a relationship in which she felt extremely dependent. Repression of her anger resulted in depression, and its periodic threat to emerge produced attacks of panic.

When Fanny attempted to put a curb on the self-aggrandizing business ventures that made her so successful, she felt identified with her childhood poverty—and this in turn filled her with self-loathing. She became depressed. This made her momentarily content and dependent on Benny, who was "always loyal." But the price of this contentment was too high. The depressions were becoming intolerable. When she gave in to her expansive nature and made big business deals, the gap between her and Benny widened: she became enraged by his inertia and her inability to move him. Pam the cat even seemed to exhibit a kind of feline indifference, and Fanny's self-hate and emerging rage produced anxiety attacks and panic. She was in a no-win trap.

If she left Benny she would be alone, and no amount of money made that tolerable. Getting along alone required self-esteem she didn't have.

If she met someone else, he might turn out to be a Benny.

If she met a tycoon like herself or a celebrity, he "wouldn't want me." "But even if he did," she says, "he'd turn out to be a bastard. That's what it takes to reach the top—I know people like that."

Is there a way out of her dilemma? Fanny must change her standards and her expectations. Measures of people—herself, Benny, and others—must undergo profound changes. Her own humanity must be broadened and developed. She must extricate herself from her mother's brainwashing and her own early triumph fantasies. She must learn to relate on a less superficial level and come to realize the extent to which she has been a victim of the fame-and-money myth. She must review her childhood, learn to value and love the child she was, and cease being embarrassed by her roots. Only then will she lose her cynicism and gain enough compassion to make it possible for her to like, and even to love, herself and people, as well as a cat. Her relationship with her father must be understood in all its ramifications, so that she no longer sees herself as damaged by her connection to him. Indeed, an expression of real acceptance and respect for him as a decent human being—let alone love for him—would be a sign of considerable progress. If Fanny could transfer some emotional investment from Pam the cat to Benny and to other persons and people, she might be on the road to a dilution of cynicism and hopelessness and an increase of esteem for the human condition, people, and self.

Self-effacing/Detached

They seem to have much in common. They appear shy and retiring, but for one it's not caring enough to become involved and for the other it's being too self-effacing to speak up. But they are both on the quiet side and so may take to each other. The compliant person looks attractive because he/she readily acquiesces in the detached person's judgments and therefore seems like a trouble-free partner. The detached person appears silent and strong—with reserves of intellect and wisdom—a fitting oak for the clinging vine. Each provides an unconscious foil for the other's needs—self-effacement for the detached person, and detachment and pseudo-expansiveness for the effacing person. But this seemingly neat lock can result in the most paralyzing kind of inertia. The detached person will not invest enough emotion to make decisions and get involved. The compliant partner is frightened of assertive choices, decisions, and acts.

The detached person, leaning on truth and principle, may be forced to be the decider and supporter and may well resent this role, feeling terribly coerced and put upon. He/she will also resent the clinging demand for demonstrations of love or support by the needy partner and will feel even more inundated than if his/her partner were an expansive narcissist. Sometimes the detached person will show arrogance and resentment for a partner who always needs people, and contempt of the partner's efforts to achieve popularity or lovability.

The compliant person, on the other hand, feels fooled. The strong, silent partner is someone who steadfastly *resists* playing sturdy oak for the compliant partner's clinging vine. The compliant partner feels chilled and isolated, rebuffed and rejected repeatedly; he/she cannot understand the partner's need for privacy and seclusion.

Expressions of pain on the part of the compliant partner are extremely abrasive to the detached partner. But the "silent treatment" inflicts extreme cruelty on the effacing partner, especially one who has more than the usual morbid dependency. She/he suffers most at the hands of a partner whose integrity, principle, and freedom from involvement are considered more valuable than people. But even though the compliant partner feels resentment at such treatment, he/she maintains great respect for an independence and integrity that the effacing partner knows is personally unachievable.

The detached person will stay in such a relationship only because of paralysis due to resignation. If the detached partner takes on a hint of expansiveness—if, for example, he or she gets a promotion, with a resulting rush of self-esteem—this expansive surge may carry him (or her) out of the relationship.

The morbidly dependent partner may stay only because "it is so cold out there," but he/she will crave much more attention from the partner and will make many claims. These will be thwarted, and the dependent partner may then be enraged. However, this alternation of claim and denial rarely becomes sadomasochistic. Detached people do not make the best sadomasochistic partners—sadomasochism calls for too much closeness. If a more domineering partner is readily available, the compliant person may leave. In general, a self-effacing/detached lock is not the strongest one, but it may be permanent nonetheless, on the basis of detached apathy and compliant, dependent fear.

Mel and Linda

"The truth? He could dance. That was it, stupid as it sounds now, thirty years later. His dancing; a camel's hair coat he wore; smoked a cigarette like Humphrey Bogart—please don't laugh at me, but that's what actually hooked me. I thought of it a number of times."

"She had a nice figure—really a great figure and face also. Like she just came off one of those billboards—you remember, the girl who smokes Camels or something. Guess today the kids would call her 'cool.' Looked good in a sweater—like Lana Turner. Besides, I was nearly thirty. Time to get married. We were the same religion. Wasn't so bad all these years after all."

"Maybe not for him. For me it's been bad—bad all the way. We've spent a lifetime with nothing in common. He's never even noticed, but we haven't got a single interest together—not even the kids. He couldn't care less. Sports and TV are all that ever interested him. I like music, the ballet. Can't even say I like *him*, I really don't. Sex has been nothing for years. Only thinks of himself, anyway. Nobody in my family ever got a divorce—nobody. I just can't see it. I guess I do have some feeling for him, not even for *him*—for us—for the family. Maybe it's all a fairy tale, but I couldn't walk out. Too many years have passed—I guess it's a way of life."

Investigation confirmed what is already fairly obvious. He was a resigned man who shied away from deep relationships. Detachment was his watchword. He had gone through life in a sort of semianesthetic state, avoiding feelings of almost any kind. Though it turned out that he had considerable intelligence, his alienation from feelings, and resignation, condemned him to a lifetime of mechanical, rote living. This included a minor, undemanding government job in which virtually no decisions ever had to be made. He was further anesthetized by a television addiction, and what excitement he experienced occurred vicariously through his passive viewer's interest in sports.

She was an essentially self-effacing, dependent, conforming person who in later life had rebelled somewhat and now experienced her disappointments and anger on a conscious level. She too suffered from considerable resignation, and this, combined with poor self-esteem, contributed to an overwhelming sense of hopelessness and futility. She had—but did not believe it—intelligence and ability; her poor self-image made her cling to the status quo as she knew it. She was resigned to her position with him, making it almost impossible to extricate herself from a relationship that provided her with minimal emotional nourishment.

In fact, their relationship had been initiated as a result of cultural mythology and influence, and had been sustained largely as a result of cultural conformity. She, particularly, had been thoroughly brainwashed by romantic myths and actually pictured herself dancing her way through life with this strong, Bogart-like man. Of course, he was only in costume and was no more like the character Bogart played than Bogart himself. He backed into the relationship largely because it was the thing to be done but, as with most else in his life, with little enthusiasm. Their common religion did nothing to extend a few weeks of fantasized glamour and fun; soon the reality of mundane tasks, bills to be paid, etc., made them feel mired in mechanical living and tedium.

Despite great disappointment, she had a feeling for their history together, and because of this and her dependency, her low self-esteem and cultural and familial convention, she "stuck." He stuck because he was too alienated to really know that anything was wrong and too resigned to the status quo. Chances are that he also was trying to preserve their history together from the rupture of divorce, although this effort was largely an unconscious one on his part.

SADOMASOCHISM

Sadomasochism in its broadest context—that is, outside of and including the purely sexual area—may be found in conjunction with any of the other locks we have been discussing. Since it is probably, in one or another of the many forms it takes, the most prevalent lock of all, we may think of it as a master lock. Elements of sadomasochistic relating occur in superficial, short-lived relationships as well as in sustained, close relationships. They are common in parent/child relating, among siblings, between mates, and among professional colleagues.

Generally, I agree with Karen Horney's conceptualizations regarding this mechanism. Neither she nor I feel that sadomasochism is instinctual in nature. We certainly do not believe that women are basically and instinctively masochistic, or that men are basically and instinctively sadistic. Indeed, it is my belief that human beings are almost entirely instinct-free and that our behavior, depending on degree of health, is either dictated by neurosis—by strong needs and desires—or is the result of internal conflicts and anxieties of which we are consciously unaware, or is the result of free choice.

Both Horney and I agree that sadomasochism is a neurotic form of behavior. I believe that sadism and its opposite number, masochism, are, like so many other neurotic adaptations, largely outgrowths of cultural influences and dictates.

Sadomasochism in this context must be viewed as more than a narrowly sexual dynamic. Sadomasochism describes a way of relating that may or may not include sexual or any kind of physical abuse; what interests us most here is the way it is manifested in the emotional area of a relationship.

In sadomasochistic relating the masochist plays the role of dependent, devoted, weak, selfless (without a self), compliant, supplicating disciple. The sadist plays the role of masterful, knowing, independent, sometimes rebellious, domineering manipulator.

In fact, this is role-playing. Each partner feels inwardly weak, vulnerable, often deadened, very dependent. Both attempt to strengthen feelings that are often too weak to be felt otherwise by inflicting and receiving pain, by living through each other, and by manipulating each other. They are, in fact, chronically, morbidly dependent on each other; the duration of their relationship is directly proportional not only to their need to mitigate deadness but also to their dependency. And the greater the emotional deadness each feels, the greater is his or her dependency or desire to join forces with another, *alive* self. The *intensity* of sadomasochistic interplay, as well as its duration, is also directly proportional to deadness of feelings.

An exchange of roles also takes place periodically in a sadomasochistic relationship, something that seems to freshen the relating process in an attempt to retain the stimulating effects of pain or misery for either tormentor or tormented. Sometimes there are periods during which both partners play out sadistic roles in an attempt to experience feelings and in a competition for that role. Should either partner, however, fail to take on the opposite role when required, the relationship will fall apart. It also ends if either partner changes or grows healthy enough to refuse to continue the interplay.

Sadomasochistic interplays in many relationships may be so

subtle and muted as to be hardly detectable. There may be just the quietest type of bullying or manipulating or begging—for a fur coat, for instance—or the kind of papa/daughter or mama/son role-playing one occasionally sees between married adults. Sadomasochism may be experienced through who governs the money and how it is used—in both personal and professional relationships—through who makes the decisions, through who establishes rewards and restrictions, through who yells and who cringes. And its operation can be so subtle that many of us are never aware of how pervasive the sadomasochistic relationship is.

Why is sadomasochism so common in so many relationships in our society, even in those where it is not the principal theme? I believe we have to look to our culture for that answer. Consider our early childhood experiences with reward and punishment. A parent rewards with pleasure and punishes through pain—by depriving the child of pleasure, of his or her company. Such experiences inevitably result in repressed anger, feelings of injustice, and vindictive fantasies ("I'll make them sorry they treated me that way") that can be translated into action later on. Early feelings of helplessness eventually are compensated for by manipulation of others.

Then, too, many cultural influences—such as feelings about money, competition, sex stimulation addiction, and others that I'll discuss later—have the effect of deadening sensation, making the individual seek vicarious, synthetic aliveness, usually through competition. Sadomasochism is a natural blood brother of competition; one feeds the other. Triumph in competition is, after all, vindictive: a great part of the satisfaction is in feeling the failure of the vanquished adversary in contrast with one's own elevation.

It is also my belief that people who are largely incompatible, especially in terms of character structure, tend to drift toward sadomasochism. They are taught to despise (or at least to denigrate) whatever is different from themselves; and when they cannot find satisfaction in a relationship with someone unlike themselves, they use sadomasochism to punish the "different" partner, on whom they blame their own frustration at the failure of the relationship.

Those people who, for one or another reason, cannot extricate themselves from such a relationship (e.g., because of convention, economics, or morbid dependency) use sadomasochism to further bind them. In short, sadomasochism becomes their closeness and their relationship.

But I feel that the main function of sadomasochism is the attempt to use it as a comprehensive solution to the cultural competition/cooperation conflict, so as to mitigate the anxiety this conflict produces. Sadism is felt as satisfying competitive needs. Masochism is felt as satisfying cooperative needs. Since sadomasochistic partners periodically change roles, some measure of inner equilibrium is established as each need is satisfied; the relationship is neurotically served and therefore tends to be sustained. Even when the couple are no longer in physical proximity, their sadomasochistic interplay may be sustained. I have seen any number of relationships in which the masochist finally breaks away; then for years the sadist takes on the role of masochist as he supplicates for him/her to return, which he/she sadistically refuses to do. Thus, the relationship continues even as they remain physically apart.

This is not surprising considering the underlying forces involved. Human beings cling desperately to life. They will do almost anything to mitigate feelings of inner deadness. The pseudo-aliveness of sadomasochism is a poor and even destructive substitute for real aliveness born of a healthy struggle to relate constructively. But even pseudo-aliveness exerts a powerful force in a cemetery of dead feelings.

Mom

She is an old lady now, eighty-five; her husband died ten years ago. She depended on him for just about everything. She had been naïve, gentle, and utterly compliant. In her time and generation she was considered the perfect housewife and mother. Nobody remembers her ever raising her voice, let alone getting angry. Even her crying was done quietly; nevertheless, her children had seen her weep a good deal through the years.

There had been hard times. Her husband, George, was domineering, often self-centered, and seemingly negligent of her needs, which were largely for attention and tenderness. George had been a distinct force and a powerful presence throughout his life, and she had seen him manipulate people all the time—benevolently, "for their good." She was in the background—liked by everyone—passive, nice, doing whatever she was supposed to, like raising good future citizens.

The children did turn out well—financially too, and therefore they were able to take good care of her after George was gone. For a while it seemed she would get along despite the fact that she missed him and his directions. But then she seemed to age very quickly, and fell all the time. Her children thought she should have twenty-four-hour care. Physical examination, incidentally, revealed nothing. Despite her age she seemed to be in perfect health.

Since she seemed most comfortable in her own apartment, it was arranged for her to have companions, who also cleaned, shopped, and cooked. A total of four women were involved—at least one of whom was always there so that Mom was never alone. She stopped falling.

At first things went exceedingly well. The women loved Mom. She loved them, and they also loved each other. Everybody cooperated, and Mom's children were happy. But this didn't last. The ladies in attendance began to bicker. There were complaints about money, schedules, mostly about one another. They constantly called Mom's children, denouncing one another, each claiming to be more concerned about Mom than the others. Then Mom began to complain, first about one, then about another—sometimes two were all right and the other two were "no good"; then it would switch back again. Each week Mom had a different favorite, and she seemed unable or unwilling to love all four at the same time as she had when they first came. When it was suggested that different people be hired, she objected adamantly. She could not tolerate any change at this time. Besides, they had become "like family to me," even though there were always at least two that she hated.

Questioning both the women and Mom soon revealed to the children that gentle Mom had suddenly developed a capacity not only for hatred but also for Machiavellian mischief and manipulation. It was she who was behind the whole breakdown—telling stories about each of the women to the others, pitting one against the other, praising here and condemning there, using favoritism and connection to the children as rewards and potential punishment.

Investigation into the distant past was not easy, but adroit conversations with Mom and with other old relatives were instructive. Mom had not always been "a naïve innocent." Indeed, as a child she had been capable of considerable envy, jealousy, and manipulation for family status in a family in which sibling rivalry flourished.

Mom was probably overtly expansive, narcissistic, and vindictive up to the time of her marriage at age seventeen. This dynamic character solution was very difficult to sustain for a woman in our culture in those years. Mom apparently repressed her expansiveness and consciously identified with her self-effacing, dependent trend at that time, or soon after her marriage. Through George, her husband, she could vicariously live out her repressed expansiveness. Their relationship was largely sadomasochistic: he manipulating her, she submitting to the manipulation and living vicariously through him. When they switched roles, she made great use of her ability to generate guilt; this made *him* suffer. When he died, the sweet-Mom role was not enough anymore. He was gone and the children were off living their own lives. She had no one through whom to live vicariously anymore, no one to manipulate (as she had manipulated her brothers and sisters), and no means of self-glorification through motherhood or passive martyrdom. And perhaps, after the mourning period was over, she was bored.

The children at first thought that Mom's newfound querulousness and abrasiveness were part of old age—"a kind of senility." They weren't. Mom needed drama. She needed stimulation. She needed focus and she needed attention, and she found the way to get them all.

She became the center of concern and attention for her ladies-in-waiting and her children. Exhibiting the skills she had shown in the sibling rivalry of her childhood, she masterfully manipulated them all—and now she had the added advantage of being able to produce guilt easily because of the "helplessness" of old age and her history as the angel-martyr mother she had played for most of her life. Now, she played out the roles of both sibling and queen mother: everyone danced to her tune, and she was thus furnished with an ongoing, successful, exciting melodrama, with herself cast in the role of perpetual star. None of the supporting players was aware of what was going on, but even if one had been, radical change in the scenario would probably not have been possible. However, insight will help them not to feel guilty and to accept the situation compassionately.

Mary, Arthur, Jimmie, Peter, and Pops

Mary and Arthur never got along from the time Arthur was born. Mary was "not proud of it"—after all, Arthur is her son—but it's always been that way. They fought about everything. As far as she is concerned, he has always been obstinate, demanding, aggressive, and hostile to her. Her younger son, Jimmie, on the other hand, was always "good as gold." "From the beginning—just as if he were never there at all—never any trouble." Jimmie is three years younger than Arthur.

Peter is Mary's husband. He works for Pops, Mary's father, and Pops has always run the show. Pops is a "self-made man," which means that he has accumulated a great deal of money from his manufacturing business and shrewd real-estate deals.

Mary is an only child. She was the apple of Pops's eye from the moment she was born. In fact, Pops stopped paying much attention to Fay, his wife and Mary's mother, from the time of Mary's birth. Pops was both father and husband to her—"except sexually, of course," Mary says. Yet she remembers the seductive nightgowns he used to buy her, starting at about the same time her periods began. And there were always other lavish, inappropriate gifts, like expensive watches, earrings, rings, and quite grownup dresses.

When Mary's son Arthur was born, Pops's attentions to Mary changed. Arthur took Mary's place as his favorite. In no time at all he saw Arthur as the extension of himself. Arthur would do all the things he hadn't been able to. "After all, how much can you do in one lifetime?" he said. Arthur would go to school. He would become a great lawyer. He would have fine clothes, fast cars, all of it—and through Arthur Pops could live several lifetimes at least. It must be remembered that inflicting pain is not the only manifestation of sadism; manipulation of others and vicarious living through them are also very important forms of sadism.

Mary and Arthur's relationship grew worse, and she consulted a psychiatrist. In a short time, it became apparent that Pops, Arthur, and Mary had a great deal in common, as did Peter and Jimmie. The latter were easygoing, almost indifferent at times, liked by everyone, and easily pleased. Pops, Arthur, and Mary were aggressive, competitive, self-aggrandizing, opinionated, and often arrogant. They usually got what they wanted, and they almost always wanted a great deal. In short, Mary hated those aspects of herself that she saw in Arthur, and it was easier to hate Arthur than herself. This kind of hatred for one's own characteristics, projected onto somebody else, often takes the form of sadistic ploys to rid oneself of the symptoms and pain of self-hate, even as one "enjoys" the pseudo-aliveness that comes of inflicting pain on a victim.

In therapy it became apparent that Pops's money had helped Mary create a family mystique, a self-image of special status—indeed, one of a kind of royalty. Mary's mother was not of the blood, so to speak. She had only *married* Pops. Mary, on the other hand, was of his blood, which made her at least a crown princess if not Pops's rightful queen. After all, Pops had always treated her accordingly and had neglected his own wife, from the time his crown princess was born. Mary identified with Pops and saw her own husband and younger son ("Jimmie is just like Peter") as she did her mother—as consorts who were there to help the royal couple, Pops and herself.

Mary denied sexual feelings for her father, but somehow was always attracted to "strong men like him" and had a very poor sex life with Peter. Indeed, Peter had largely fulfilled his function by making Mary pregnant. Pops wanted a grandson. In the sexual sense, Peter had been Pops's surrogate. Arthur was something else again. To Pops he was Mary's male counterpart, his own extension, a crown prince (so much more potent a figure than a crown princess). Pops no longer seemed to need the sexual stimulation of Mary's femininity, so Arthur supplanted Mary in the line of succession.

Obviously the setting was tailor-made for intense sibling rivalry between mother and son, which would in turn lay the groundwork for future sadism on Arthur's part. It helped that Mary was very young when she gave birth to Arthur. It also helped that she was an only child. Pops helped a great deal, too. Mary's father had become her husband in part. Her son had become her sibling rival for royal favor and royal power. They both saw Mary's mother, Peter, and Jimmie as nice, nonthreatening, almost useless drones. Though I had no actual verification, I theorized that Mary's mother, husband, and younger son are repressing vast storehouses of intense rage, which will provide fuel for every kind of antagonistic relating. Mary and her family have much to work out in order for real change to take place.

INVIDIOUS FRIENDSHIPS

Let me close this section on neurotic locks by discussing an off-shoot of sadomasochism and one of the most common kinds of friendships found in our competitive society. The central dynamic of this "friendship" is the neurotic satisfaction born of making the other person envious of one's own achievements, position, possessions, or prestige. I call such a relationship an invidious friendship; although its invidiousness is seldom apparent on the surface, this competitive friendship is largely based on making the friend envious. The invidious partner derives satisfaction from having achieved a higher position on the hierarchical ladder than his envious friend. Proof of his having achieved it is the envy of his friend. Generating envy may or may not be coupled with other dynamics that hold the friendship together, including the usual neurotic locks as well as constructive commonality of interests and values. But how central invidiousness is to these relationships can be seen because when this force is diluted or removed by change or growth in one or both friends, the relationship is often terminated.

Since money plays an enormous role in our culture, its use to produce envy among friends is epidemic. Money is used in more than talk about "killings," "smart manipulations," "salaries," "bonuses," etc.; its presence is also demonstrated by material acquisitions of all kinds, vacations taken, bragging about leisure time—"how little I work these days," etc.

Invidiousness starts at an early age and, I believe, is initiated by parents; children observe and imitate their parents, with whom they identify, and they are also *taught* by their parents, who unwittingly transmit their satisfaction in having their children possess more than other children do—talent, looks, and intelligence, more education, a better school, a better team. Children are used for hierarchical parental status even as they themselves are inculcated into the process of making their little peers envious. In adolescence, this process surges forward in all kinds of competitions involving athletics, getting into clubs and the "right" schools, and so on. There is also the chronic activity of ranking, in which each child verbally attempts to put his/her friends down.

The invidious process uses sadism, as do sadomasochistic relationships, but masochism tends to be lacking in an invidious friendship, as is the refined dance of sadomasochism, which involves practiced responses and willing switching of roles. Sadomasochism is most common among couples living together; invidiousness is most common among friends and is often found in couples who act as teams to make other couples and families envious.

It must be understood that many people enjoy telling others about their windfalls and successes, not to create envy, but rather to share openly the joy that they feel. This is the antithesis of the invidious process. One is used to share and to bring together. The other is used to deplete. But "open sharing" is often misinterpreted as "bragging" by people who engage in invidious practices themselves and who suffer from chronic attacks of envy.

The invidious process can become malignant enough to blot out all other aspects of a relationship—at which point the relationship itself may become painful enough to force one or both partners to terminate it. Many invidious relationships grind down in this way, but often, in an unconscious last-ditch effort to produce stimulation and interest, one partner will attack the other, hoping to score a vindictive triumph. Instead of simply reminding his friend of his own promotion, he says, "I understand they promoted Al and they didn't promote you." The relationship will then end with a bang, consisting of insults and hurts, rather than just petering out. In these cases, old friends go away licking their wounds, feeling that they have been unjustifiably attacked and hurt, having no idea how they participated in the debacle.

LOCKS AND KEYS

In the case histories we have discussed we can readily see the high degree of complexity and overlapping that take place in all human relationships. In actuality, while each case highlights particular aspects of our discussion, a complete analysis of each one would demonstrate many of the dynamics described in this book. Just as none of these case histories is an illustration, pure and simple, of the locks discussed, so the locks themselves never exist in pure form. I describe them only to indicate general and possible directions neurotic relating takes. So-called potentially workable locks— for example, a relationship between a self-effacing and an expansive partner—do not work well if the couple have nothing in common. A relationship can also be complicated by undue morbid dependency in self-effacing, compliant people, undue resignation in detached people, and arrogant vindictiveness and perfectionism in expansive people. And relationships can be further complicated by a host of other factors. Any self-hate felt by either partner and traded mutually strengthens the lock position because it leads to sadomasochism, the cultural super-lock. The phenomenon of transference also tightens locks when current relationships become confused with past unfinished business.

But let us not forget the role of health and prevention also. Although a neurotic lock is a relating process locked in by the unconscious needs and drives of the relating partners, even the sickest of such partners has healthy assets, too. The same is true even in the sickest relationships.

So it is not unusual—even as locking takes place—to see an *unlocking* process taking place. Here each partner helps the other, even as each helps himself/herself, to *dilute* the compulsive power of character trends and solutions instead of working to preserve it. Unlocking is not easy: it is a process full of emotional storms that can be generated by crisis, by psychoanalytic intervention, by loss (of a loved one or a job), by a major change in status quo (a promotion, a move) and it can involve painful emotional reactions, including depression and anxiety. Some relationships collapse under threat of dissolution of the lock, some become more strongly locked than ever, and others unlock—and continue toward greater health the rest of both partners' lives.

Whether or not unlocking can take place at all—and whether it should—depends to a great extent on the people involved. People of different main solutions often do not understand each other and feel they are of a different species. Their experiences have been different and are perceived differently. Their fear of hidden character trends within themselves is often projected as contempt of a partner in whom that trend is a main solution. Transcending those complications is only possible for people who struggle all their lives for compassion for themselves and for each other. And transcendence is much more difficult if the relating partners are *extremely* self-effacing, *extremely* expansive, *extremely* detached.

Preventing the locking process is something that can take place only relatively. Since we are *all* neurotic to some extent, some locking must take place. But much of it can be prevented. What is mainly required is time and patience and a willingness—on both partners' parts—to get to know each other before any kind of permanent commitments take place.

Most people, if they stop to listen to themselves, will have a sense of what is good and bad for them. Such a sense takes time and patience to develop, and interlocking can begin with our very first meeting; neurotic processes do not wait. But listening to our feelings and struggling to wait until we know each other may dilute neurotic processes.

As we have seen in all the case histories we've examined so far, some locks seem harder to unlock than others, and other locks seem less confining, more tenable, than some. What makes some locks work, and some untenable, are the *qualitative* measures of human relating. In the following section we will examine and discuss forces in our emotional lives that influence the outcome of human relationships.

III

THE SUBSTANCE
OF RELATING

DEPTH

In this section we will further examine our interpersonal lives in qualitative terms. It is not enough to describe relationships as adversary, cooperative, or antagonistic. Nor is it enough to describe them as locks of one character type with another. For a close-up understanding we must examine the close-up substance of relationship: the way people feel about each other. We must ask questions about depth of feeling, openness, tenderness, trust, intimacy, kindness, and other qualities.

We might say that up to this point we have been looking at relationships from a macroscopic, or global, point of view. In this section we involve ourselves with the microscopic substance.

The depth of a relationship is not always directly proportional to its duration. Many sustained relationships are essentially shallow, and there are ones of short duration in which deep relating has taken place. In shallow relationships—including relationships between people who work together, socialize, or even live together— little exchange really takes place, and as a result mutual impact is minimal. Change occurring as a result of relating is likewise minimal. The people involved may meet, but they continue separately, as if they haven't met at all, since each registers very little emotional change resulting from contact with the other. The two individuals may be in each other's presence for as much as years at a time, but each is furniture to the other—pleasant or abrasive, but inspiring little emotional flow or investment.

Of course, there is no absolutely superficial or absolutely deep relationship. But there are dynamics that determine relative depth in relationships and that provide standards for this kind of relative differentiation typing by descriptive criteria.

Sharing of information, ideas, and feelings is an important aspect of deeper relating. This is especially true of information and feelings about oneself and each other—lack of self-confidence, anger, irritability at the partner, whatever. These feelings must be expressed truly, without duplicity or affectation. This is information shared for the sake of closeness and real exchange, rather than for the sake of manipulation to get what one wants or to impress.

Depth is also related to emotional investment. In a deep relationship the partners have *strong* feelings about each other. Deep relating does not preclude sick relating—in a deep relationship, sick or healthy, each relating partner cares deeply about the condition of the other. In a healthy deep relationship awareness and reactivity to the other person's condition are connected to caring for the other's well-being. In a sick deep relationship (of which sadomasochistic and antagonistic relating are characteristic) the individual usually perceives the partner's condition largely in terms of how well that condition can be exploited. In a healthy deep relationship there is at least some sharing of problems, both mutual and individual. The phrase "that's your problem" is characteristic of more superficial contact.

Of course, deeper relationships are also characterized by the process of increasing mutual interests and mutual investments, in people—friends, family—as well as in ideas and activities, as time goes on.

But from my point of view, the single most important characteristic of a deep relationship is a shared personal history. The partners' history together, whatever its length, is of prime importance to them. Shared history has little value to people who are involved only superficially, regardless of the length of time they have been together. Reverence for these parts of their life's experience that they shared—problems, frustrations, tragedies, accomplishments, change, growth, hurts (including ones perpetrated on each other), joys, exchanges with other people—is crucial in deep relationships. This emotional investment invariably indicates considerable commitment in the relationship.

As I've said earlier, history involves time, and a sense of history is therefore more likely to be found in sustained relationships. But people sometimes have long histories that are relatively meaningless to them. There are others whose histories are not as long but who feel very strongly about the past that they've shared. So the *value* placed on shared history is as important as the history itself in determining the depth of a relationship.

Usually, a deep relationship is more difficult to extricate oneself from. On the other hand, an in-depth relationship generally provides more interest and greater possibilities for meaningful exchange. Shallow relating is usually found where locks are relatively weak, so that *breaking* a lock does not ordinarily lead to great anxiety.

Lionel and Lisa

This couple was seen by their friends as "glittering, beautiful, fun-loving." Some people used the word *charismatic* to describe them. When asked how things were with them, their inevitable answer was "Great!" They both loved clothes, drove the "right" car, and lived in a chic apartment house on Manhattan's Upper East Side.

They were known to be overtly critical and judgmental of people who were not good-looking or particularly successful by cultural standards. *They* had gone to the "right" schools and usually saw Broadway plays on or as close to opening night as possible. Lionel spent a great deal of his time at business—he was an executive in a large firm. Lisa spent much time shopping and getting her hair and nails done. They gave large cocktail parties every three or four months and ate out frequently with friends, of whom they had many. In actuality, few of their "friends" knew very much about them except that they were good-looking, fun, and obviously successful. The trappings of their success included many weekends skiing, winter vacations in the best-known warm-weather spots, and summer vacations in the Hamptons, where they gave large cocktail parties every few weeks. They could not remember inviting "just a few friends over for dinner," and they took pains to avoid any kind of "heavy talk," on the few occasions when they ate out alone.

There was just one thing wrong with this picture of chic success: Lionel and Lisa were having trouble with each other. They sought psychological counseling because their fights were becoming more frequent and more vitriolic, and having parted several times, they were now thinking of making their separation permanent. They had been married about ten years, and, as Lisa blurted out, "The truth is, it's never been good." During their consultation with me, they continually blamed each other for their difficulties, neither wishing to accept responsibility and both making claims on the other for understanding.

The fact is, there was very little openness, tenderness, trust or intimacy, caring or kindness between them, or between them and anyone else. They each had a very long history—going back to their early teens—of posing and pretense. I found no significant evidence of any real interest in another person, in people in general, or in the world at large; they seemed to care only for their immediate surroundings and how they themselves were affected by them.

This is an example of two highly narcissistic, shallow people who affected a pose for the outside world but who had very little tolerance for each other. Their relationship to outside people was utterly superficial and so was each one's relationship to the other. Caring and kindness were almost nonexistent. They had very little interest in past history and in fact used history between them only to seek further evidence for recrimination. "Do you remember," said Lisa to Lionel, "the time two years ago when you forgot my birthday?" Interestingly, their sexual lives were satisfactory in terms of arousal and response, but neither Lionel nor Lisa was aware of any love or tenderness during sex. This is often true of alienated people who function sexually but for whom this function is not in any way linked to other feelings. We can theorize, though, that, in view of their great similarity, and their high degree of narcissism and alienation, they got through the barrier of antagonism sexually by seeing each other as mirror images of themselves. Thus, in effect they engaged in masturbatory or solitary sex, even though it took place together.

Lisa and Lionel had, in fact, been engaged in an antagonistic relationship for some time and did not seem to be inclined toward other possibilities. They came to see me, not to get help, but to use me to support them in their onslaught on each other and to win me over to believing that each was right in hating the other. Lionel and Lisa have a narcissistic/narcissistic lock on each other, and the shallowness of their relationship precludes any exchange that would enhance either of them. On the other hand, they might be able to extricate themselves from the lock more easily because of the superficiality of the relationship.

I do not know whether they parted company or continued on an antagonistic basis. Antagonism can keep people together in a state of mutual pseudo-aliveness for a lifetime. Unlike basic sado-masochism, an exchange of roles between victim and victimizer is not common in such a relationship.

KINDNESS

Kindness in a relationship is not a function of sentiment or idealization but one of significant practical value. The fact is that levels of kindness, including lack of it, play an important role in relationships and are invariably connected to all other dynamics central to the process, giving us a good deal of information quickly.

Kindness does more than simply make things pleasant in a relationship. Kindness makes it easier to deal with the kind of mutual frustration born of inevitable arrhythmias and communication breakdowns. It also adds immeasurably to the closeness and mutual support felt as life's inevitable difficulties are faced singly and together. Kindness helps to dilute pride; it helps partners "forgive and forget." Genuine kindness, the real thing, also helps to establish an ambience in which mutual trust can flourish.

In this context, cruelty is more than lack of kindness. It characterizes a relationship marked by one or more of a number of chronic assaults by each partner on the other. The following are common cruel maneuvers: recrimination, disparagement, discouragement, producing frustration, teasing, verbal and physical assault, and vindictiveness, all forms of chronic mutual sabotage, broken promises and contracts, lying, setting up double-bind situations, creating embarrassment and every conceivable maneuver designed to create self-hate, hopelessness, and to destroy self-esteem, confidence, creativity, happiness, and joy. Many vindictive people are particularly ingenious at picking up vulnerable areas and making creative use of them in the service of cruelty. Two such people are capable of producing unbelievably ingenious scenarios for mutual torture.

At a slightly less malevolent point on the kindness scale is indifference. Indifference may be a form of conscious cruelty, but it may also be an expression of simply not caring. Of course, indifference—whether it is contrived or relatively benign—is felt as malignant neglect by people who are particularly helpless or dependent. Motive or lack of motive in no way mitigates the pain of neglect they feel. So what may not be *meant* cruelly is often perceived as cruelty on the receiving end.

Slightly kinder than indifference is what I call *passive caring*. Passive caring consists of understanding, empathy, sympathy, and sensitivity to the other person's sensibilities and needs. This borders on active support but is not quite the same thing. Feelings for and about another person—especially when they are expressed and when they serve no personal motive—can be supportive; some people might consider such expressions active kindness, but they require too little energy, time, and self-investment to quite meet the criterion I have in mind.

Active caring consists of, and is measured by, the energy, time, and dedication one person contributes to the other. This is more than lip service and motivation (self-satisfaction doesn't matter). This kind of caring is measured by how much help is given to the other person, not by what one gets out of giving oneself. My father once told me that the Talmud measured friendship and goodness by the act of goodness (or lack of it) itself, rather than by the specifics of motivation. Thus, a person is measured not by *why* he gives to a friend but by the fact that he gives and that the friend benefits.

When someone says to me, "She doesn't care about me anymore," what he is often really saying is, "She's broken our contract; she won't support my self-idealizations anymore." This has nothing to do with *caring* and is a complication of an adversary relationship.

Deep, active caring—what I mean when I speak of kindness—involves a willingness to sacrifice one's own priorities and preferences in order to satisfy the needs of one's relating partner. I am not talking about seeking glory through martyrdom here. I am talking about a deep, caring, relating process in which one partner, at least, feels enough self-esteem so that threat of self-depletion is not an issue—the kind of relationship in which a parent works so that a child can go to school, not because the parent glories in self-sacrifice, not with any feeling that the child "owes" him something, not with any feeling of bitterness at the child. This kind of relating is always characterized by an ongoing struggle to understand the other person's aspirations, proclivities, assets, limitations, vulnerabilities. It precludes ruthlessness in the service of self. Kindness is most often to be found in a creative relationship—the antithesis of a lock. So it should be obvious that kindness always works against the neurotic locking process and helps build constructive relationships.

DEGREES OF REACTIVITY

Interaction is the elemental stuff of all relationships, but *reactivity* in this context is a special kind of interaction in which reaction to the other person's moods, feelings, tastes, choices, decisions, and actions takes precedence over reaction to one's own inner workings. Indeed, the reaction to each other can become more important than the people themselves. In *high* degrees of reactivity, which have reached malignant proportion, the investment in a lifelong reactive battle may obliterate all other interactions and feelings. As a patient of mine put it, "I am so busy reading him and responding to him that I never stop to know what I see or feel."

In reactivity, the actual exchange of feelings takes a backseat to stimulation and response. Personal values, ideas, and feelings are nullified or dulled as the individuals involved react to each other's statement without even thinking about it, as if they were responding to a conditioned reflex. Thus, in a relationship where there is a high degree of reactivity, so little real exchange of personal feelings takes place (despite much frothy explosion between both partners) that the partners may suffer from intense feelings of isolation and loneliness. And this isolation makes them seek further reactive confrontations simply to *make contact*, as a compensation for lack of personal inner constructive exchange. Thus, mutual reactions often include recriminations, vindictive tirades, and much verbalization of mutual claims.

Highly reactive people, with their zeal for bouncing off one another and their great energy for active, internecine forays, often give the impression of much aliveness and spontaneity. But their aliveness, if closely examined, turns out to be pseudo-aliveness; their spontaneity is false. The fact is that many of them are narcissistic, so much so that in the presence of others they will talk and talk about themselves and each other, believing that they and they alone are of prime interest to the world they inhabit. Their interchanges are largely repetitive rituals in which each plays out well-rehearsed roles utterly lacking in originality, creativity, or spontaneity. I have known couples who "go at each other" for hours at a time. There is no mistaking this chronic, intense process when in its presence. Its abrasive boringness affects everybody within earshot.

There are also people who, without any awareness at all, constantly change moods relative to another's mood, like helpless automatons. When she is sullen and cold, he becomes warm and obsequious. If she is warm and outgoing, he becomes sullen and cold. And so on. But reactions may exist on a much more subtle level, too—where, for example, two highly dependent, self-effacing people attempt to react to each other's opinions and desires rather than to ferret out their own. This usually leads to chronic frustration, confusion, and lack of action, since neither will offer either opinion or direction without being able to react to the other's first.

Some morbid reactivity occurs in even the healthiest relationships. All of us are neurotic to at least some extent, but the degree is important. In a very high degree of reactivity, we often see a chronic communication breakdown, for which an abrasive interacting process has malignantly displaced other possibilities. This kind of reactive interaction can have a malignantly binding effect. Regardless of whether it takes the form of self-effacing chronic mutual consultation ("What do you think?" "Well, what do *you* think?") and constant deferring to each other, or whether it is expressed in abrasive recriminations, it often serves the cause of intense morbid dependency to the point of symbiosis. In a very high degree of reactivity, people sometimes function almost as single units, having formed a neurotic lock of unparalleled bonding strength.

Pygmalion or Frankenstein? A Case of Switched Trends

They were young when they got married. She settled into domestic tranquillity and felt "quite happy being a housewife and mother." He went on to become a rich, successful businessman. They had two children, who eventually "did very well at school and in everything else, too." She was content. He became bored.

He wanted her to go back to school. She said that she had "no desire for it and no real head for it." He said she did, pointing out her ability at home, with the kids, their house, everything. He said she demonstrated amply that she was "very intelligent, logical, and organized." He said he didn't want her to waste herself. Besides, it would give him great satisfaction to watch her grow. She said she was perfectly happy with things the way they were. He insisted.

She complied. She almost always did. And he was right about her ability. She was an excellent student—indeed, she graduated *summa cum laude*. He remembered being proud of her and of himself the day she graduated. It was also the day of their wedding anniversary. That was fifteen years ago. They had been married twelve years.

He then insisted that she go on to law school. This time she needed no convincing. She complied at once, graduated with top honors, and immediately got an excellent job with a top law firm. After two years she became a partner, and after five years she had become one of the most prestigious members of her firm. She is now a famous lawyer, earns a great deal of money, and has been spoken of as a possibility for a judgeship in a high court.

The children are off on their own now and "doing okay," but things between their parents have changed radically. She gradually stopped listening to him and eventually took over their family and social life. Her business schedule seemed more demanding than his, and so they had to comply with her schedule rather than with his. They had less and less to do with his friends and colleagues and mixed more and more with hers. He says that eventually she "took over just about everything; our investments, too—everything." At first he got a kick out of it. Then he realized he couldn't stop it. "She was like a steamroller." He began to suffer from chronic mild depression.

Now they live together but don't have much to do with each other. They manage their own money and go their separate ways. He has reestablished old social ties, but they have been limited and relatively unrewarding without her. She is busy with her friends and colleagues, and finds his stuffy and boring. They visit their children together and occasionally they go out together, but mostly they are busy in their separate business lives. They haven't had sex for years. Sometimes they wonder about a divorce and have even talked about it. But they think, "What for?" and go on, resigned to things the way they are. They have both been in for consultations but have gone no further.

He says that he didn't realize how good he had it in their old life—"No good deed goes unpunished," he says. "I thought I was Pygmalion, but I created a Frankenstein monster." She says she "was a stunted child—comfortable, quiet, dry, and dead." But now, she feels, she has come to life. He's just behaving like "a spoiled little boy, used to having his way."

Here we have an example of deep reactivity occurring as the result of a monumental change in the relating process—a change engendered by switched trends (or main solutions). When they started out together, this woman's main trend was compliancy. His main trend was expansiveness. The shift in status quo awakened her repressed expansive trend; in reaction, he attempted a shift to compliancy—difficult in our culture and in the context of his business life. For a while this was the new status quo. But the role of compliancy stimulated self-hate, and he became depressed. He shifted back, but not all the way, to expansiveness. This shift brought them into a highly reactive, nontenable situation; gradually they both shifted to detachment vis-à-vis each other and to resignation concerning their life together—apart.

The emergence and blossoming of her talent are linked to her formerly repressed expansiveness but are also the product of real health. If he saw this clearly, instead of compulsively reacting to it, they would enjoy her newfound growth together—which would enhance rather than undermine their relationship. And if she really owned her own assets, she would not link closeness to him with dependency and self-effacement; she would see how their relationship is enriched by closeness. But her reactivity to him keeps her either arrogant or detached.

He equates the development of her resources as a threat to his mastery and as potential emasculation. He is really very proud of her, and also frightened of her. He has lost a sycophant and a toy, and has not yet learned to relate closely to a woman on an equitable basis. This will not be possible until he accepts his underlying dependency—his compliant trend—and is no longer afraid of its emergence.

DEGREES OF TRUST, OPENNESS, INTIMACY, AND TENDERNESS

Openness is virtually impossible without trust. Intimacy requires openness. Tenderness requires intimacy. Trust is almost meaningless without intimacy.

These dynamic forces are linked and interdependent. To be open is to be tender. To be open is to be trusting. To be open, tender, and trusting is to be intimate. They vary in degree in different relationships and in any given relationship at different times. While each dynamic quality affects the others, one may exist in greater evidence than another. Thus, a relationship may have considerable tenderness and less openness. But if any one of the four qualities is diminished, the proportion of the other qualities will lessen also. And the extent to which any one is present in a relationship is the extent to which that relationship is open, cooperative, unlocked. The combination of all these qualities is a single dynamic force; perhaps this force can be called love. Perception of

these ingredients—if indeed they can be perceived, either singu-
larly or in combination—tells us something of the quality of a
relationship.

TRUST precludes self-doubt, a feeling of unlovability, poor self-
esteem, strong feelings of vulnerability, and paranoia. Trust first
depends on one's relationship with oneself, and *then* on one's relationship with the participating partner. Real self-love and real
self-acceptance determine the potential for trust. Self-trust
predisposes us to trust others. But the same self-trust and perceptive
ability protect us from compulsive trust of those who realistically
demonstrate that trust in them would be trust destructively mis-
placed.

Trust implies a high degree of mutual comfort and a low degree
of self-defense tension. It means you have confidence in your partner not to hurt or manipulate you. You feel confident that your
partner will support your efforts at self-realization. Such support
and confidence are a function of concerned feeling for each other
and are not related to fair or foul weather, moods of any kind, favors
done or not done, or any external happening.

It is characteristic of high levels of trust that there is no concern whatsoever about equality, about sharing material goods, services, or responsibilities. Relating participants simply take what they
need spontaneously, knowing that they will not in any way be
exploited by greedy partners. It is characteristic of relationships of
low trust that there is preoccupation with sharing equally; in fact,
getting a "fair share" or equal share takes precedence over need or
desire. This mechanism unfailingly tells much about the question
of trust and is often an extension and measure of the viability of
old, unresolved sibling-rivalry forces. Another visible characteristic
of high trust, and in part an extension of lack of concern for equality, is the presence of loyalty without claims. This loyalty is a fact
of life between trusting partners; it is not based on questions like
"What did *you* do for *me* lately?" nor is it bestowed as a reward for
gifts, services, or contribution of affection. At the same time, it
must be understood that loyalty does not in any way imply efface-
ment of self. Indeed, in large part it springs from primary loyalty

and compassion for self and self-trust. High esteem, hope, and compassion for self—and the relating process in its infinite complexity—and for the relationship in question is basic to trust.

Trust leads to OPENNESS. The degree of openness is the degree of give-and-take between any two people, both qualitatively and quantitatively.

Openness precludes pretense and the constrictive, censoring effects of affectation and lack of communication. Thus, in openness all the relating selves are tapped, and this serves as a powerful antidote to stultification and boredom. Openness, it must be remembered, mainly involves discussion of the emotionally laden "private" areas of our lives. In our culture this may be very threatening indeed.

Openness involves nonjudgmental receiving and giving of information, opinions, what-have-you. In an open relationship, when one business associate asks another, "What did you think of So-and-so's memo?" it's because he *really* wants to know what his colleague thinks, not because he's trying to trap her. Indeed, this kind of receiving is perhaps the most potent and important form of human giving. Giving is also a crucial part of receiving, since the privilege of giving of self is so powerfully therapeutic to self. Therefore, receiving and giving are only ways of describing the same process or the state of being open.

Then what does openness mean in this connection? It means being in a condition to receive other people's messages, and to respond to them with *dialogue* rather than by carrying on two separate monologues. This involves free access to the use of one's perceptions, which must not be blocked by prejudice or pride of any kind.* What kinds of messages are these? These messages convey ideas, thoughts, opinions, values, and, above all, moods and feelings. Openness is not possible in a high degree of alienation, since being in touch with our own feelings is necessary if we are to

---

*It also means being free to deliver one's own messages unblocked by pride, prejudice, or fear.

make full use of our perceptions and if we are to convey our messages as well.

Our culture works against openness even as our very human selves cry out for it. Competition operates in the service of cynicism, paranoia, and closure. We are taught from an early age to mind our own business—to be secretive about money, ideas, feelings, plans, and eventually about our age, state of health, or anything personal. This lesson does not simply go away, even when we "fall in love." Unless a continuing struggle for openness takes place, intimacy cannot flourish, and a continuing inability to communicate and a sense of isolation prevail.

Repressed anger is undoubtedly one of the greatest enemies of openness. As I will explain later, in repressing anger we also repress and put out of availability other emotions, the tapping of which is necessary in order to be open.

Repressing anger also becomes an autistic process. This means that the energy used for repression is removed from use in social intercourse; the result is a sullen mood of encapsulation and removal from one's fellows. It should be obvious that experiencing anger has an opening effect, but in fact most people—even when they are conscious of angry feelings—are seldom aware that repressing or holding back anger stands in the way of openness.

In openness, in effect, we are saying continuously, "Here I am, as I really am, as I feel. No act, no frills. And I am here to accept you the way you really are, too. There is no pretense between us."

In openness, hearing occurs on all levels: what is being said, how it is being said, what is beyond what is being said. This includes nonverbal as well as verbal messages without screening. Openness includes saying it all, without censorship of any kind. The degree of openness forms the base from which intimacy and tenderness evolve and tells much about the quality of friendship between people.

INTIMACY in this frame of reference may be thought of as the kinetic extension of openness. It is the *doing* of openness—putting openness into meaningful action. While intimacy may be expressed with both words and physical moves, these are only significant if they represent feelings. Words and actions, however intimate they sound and look, have no meaning in terms of real closeness and are only perfunctory pretense and ritual if they are not rooted in and backed by feelings.

Intimacy, then, is Mary's *feeling* close to John and *feeling* John's closeness to her. She is highly receptive to her own active feelings about John and is equally receptive to sensing John's feelings for her. This dual process is reciprocated by John, and the total process involving all four feeling dynamisms constitutes intimacy.

Intimacy, as thus described, varies in degree among different people, as well as between any given couple. Feelings and moods change, and feelings of closeness do not remain static. But after a relationship has existed for a considerable period of time, the degree of closeness is often sustained with remarkably little change, even though moods and the expression of those moods may be subject to fluctuation.

There are occasions when people who have just met are capable of real intimacy. But they are rare and must not be confused with conditioned sexual responses that occur when one meets one's romantic sexual ideal. Likewise, what appear to be instant feelings of intimacy may actually be pseudo-intimacy and the result of displacement from another individual of whom the current person is a reminder. A genuine measure of intimacy is usually possible only after people have known each other long enough for their feelings to evolve and be recognized. Talking to each other and to oneself about one's feelings are indications of intimacy. But the mother of genuine intimacy is emotional investment or caring. This takes time. This takes history. This means each partner in a relationship must face himself, and the other, and each must experience himself as half of a couple as the partners cope with and react to the world and its multitudinous facets together. It means that each partner must want to know about the other.

The desire for mutual knowledge does not spring from a need to win over, to re-create in one's image, to extend one's own boundaries through subjection, to inundate, to absorb, to exploit and destroy. It does come from a wish for closeness and the rich feelings that come from such sharing. Intimacy contributes powerfully to a sense of teamwork and mutual support, offering a strong bulwark against the exigencies of life. But this valuable asset, mutual support, must not be confused with the crippling effect of morbid dependency.

Empathy and sympathy are characteristic of intimacy. It is not possible to be tuned into each other's feelings without them. But again, these must not be confused with morbid, symbiotic dependency. You are exhibiting sympathy and empathy if you pay a visit to a sick friend; but if you go home from that visit and spend a miserable evening because of it, you're confusing sympathy with excessive dependency. You are assuming the sick friend's identity. Morbid dependency is a function of narcissism: its goal is to absorb the other in order to compensate for a much weakened feeling of self. Intimacy serves the strong self that remains in its individual, separate identity and as such is able to be close to somebody else without threat to his/her separateness and unique individuality. Thus, sharing takes place without compromising separate identities.

I am reminded of a discussion I had with Dr. Bernard Berkowitz, a colleague of mine. He pointed out that people do not seem embarrassed or shocked when in the presence of people who are verbally aggressive toward one another. But they are almost always embarrassed by people who demonstrate affection toward each other by touching, kissing, or affectionate language. Why? I think that many people are embarrassed by evidence of closeness or intimacy. Fighting is seen as making distance and apartness. Affection is seen as intimacy. We live in a culture of detachment and are taught to be suspicious, wary, and embarrassed by closeness, and intimacy, and demonstrations of the latter.

The expression of TENDERNESS through speech, gesture, physical contact, and any number of creative and appropriate actions aids the cause of intimacy, and this experience is enriching for both the receiver and the giver. But although many people may *feel* tenderness, the feeling is not always translated into action. Indeed, a great number of men, particularly, may rank high in feelings of openness, intimacy, and trust, and also of tenderness, but may be severely inhibited in expressing how they feel. This is most often due to cultural pressures and confusions as to what constitutes masculinity and femininity. Some men and women fear that expressions of tenderness will make them look graceless and "corny." Though feelings of tenderness may be of high degree, inability to express them leads to the deprivation of both potential recipient and donor. And those who are reluctant to express tender feelings will never be able to do so until they feel as tender about themselves as they do about their partners.

But what about feelings of tenderness for another person? These are, after all, most important because without them all expressions and gestures are only playacting, and everyone concerned usually knows it in short order.

Genuine tenderness, unlike pseudo-tenderness, involves sensitivity to one's partner's sensibilities. This necessitates a high degree of perceptive ability as well as the motivation to know, really know, the other person and to get close enough—intimate enough—to know him or her. Real tenderness means gentle acceptance and appropriate treatment of the other person, especially of his or her sensibilities, vulnerabilities, and limitations, and of those areas of life that have significance or poignance for one's partner. Treating important areas of a person's life tenderly increases that person's respect and compassion for delicate aspects of him- or herself. The *degree* of tenderness is difficult to ascertain, especially in unexpressed feelings, but it is discernible to anyone who gets close enough to people in a relationship.

It is important to realize that tenderness is almost never one-sided. If it is, chances are it is not the real thing but is either a costuming contrivance or the empty gesture of morbid dependency or sycophancy. Real tenderness is just about always mutually felt, mutually expressed, and mutually enhanced. Its therapeutic effect, in producing greater self-acceptance, more perceptive ability, and greater openness, trust, and intimacy, is of equal benefit to both sexes of all ages.

COMMONALITY OF
CRUCIAL PRIORITIES

Nearly all of us have priorities. Many of us are not fully conscious of them, but they are nevertheless reflected in our values, choices, decisions, tastes, and styles of living. As I described in my book *Reconciliations*, conscious awareness of personal priorities can be very important in giving us back the center of gravity of our lives and helping us toward self-realization in all areas of life. Indeed, I still feel that clarifying and listing our priorities is crucial in standing up to cultural pressures and dicta, and in putting ourselves in charge of our own energy and time.

There are people who have virtually no priorities on any level, either conscious or unconscious. They usually suffer from severe alienation and live on a chaotic impulse level marked by lack of any continuum. Their relationships are usually fragmented, and impulse-ridden, lacking any real semblance of constructive exchange.

Knowing crucial priorities can be critical in assessing relationships and their constructive or destructive potential. Partners in a relationship may be said to have common priorities or divergent priorities, and when they have divergent priorities, either of two conditions may exist. Within a shared field of given priorities, they may feel differences in degree: for example, to Mary sex may be of utmost importance, while to her husband, Jack, sex has relevance but is not very important; on the other hand, for John sex is crucial, while his wife, Jane, would just as soon do without it. The other kind of divergence may be measured in terms of number of priorities that are different: of ten priorities, Jack and Mary share eight, while John and Jane share none.

Where there are marked and severe differences in crucial priorities, relationships sometimes turn out to have been cases of mistaken identity or were based on impulse decisions without any real knowledge of each other. There are rare people who sustain relationships despite critically disparate crucial priorities. They are usually fairly alienated and very detached, and though they have a kind of relationship, it is a diluted one—they spend little time together. These are people who never knew and never get to know each other, and certainly do not know each other's priorities.

Where there are no crucial priorities at all—and therefore no commonality *or* divergence of priorities—it is difficult for any kind of lock to form.

Those whose priorities are largely disparate usually suffer great unhappiness, and their time together is filled with claims, blame, and antagonism. More often than not, these couples are not consciously aware of their differences in priorities. They may very well have strong ones, but they have not discussed each other's priorities and in many cases have not consciously confronted their own.

We are talking about major priorities that affect relationships, not the multitude of interests derived from those priorities. For example, how one feels about money is a *crucial priority* that will affect decisions regarding its expenditure; these decisions are *derivative priorities*. From my experience in clinical practice I have drawn up a list of what I consider the fifteen areas of crucial priorities for people living in our society (I list them in no special order):

1. SEX

I will discuss sex (and money, too) later in terms of an indication of the condition of a relationship. But in this context we are concerned with sex or the degree of interest in sex as a priority, rather than mutual attraction or the ability to satisfy each other. For some people there is nothing in life that occupies a higher order of importance than sex. For others it is a minor activity. For some, sexual feelings, expression, and performance are equated with life itself; being satisfied sexually is one of the measures of self-esteem. For others, sex is one of many vehicles for the expression of closeness and tenderness. For still others, it is only a vehicle for potential pleasure. There are also people for whom it has almost no meaning at all, and some who want as little to do with it as possible.

2. RELIGION

Whether two relating partners have the same or different religions is not as important as the value they put on religion. Difficulties that arise from belonging to different religions are accentuated when the intensity of religious belief varies from partner to partner. These difficulties become even more complicated when there is great pride investment either in one's religious feelings or in one's particular religion—which can be quite as damaging as the different religious beliefs and activities themselves.

3. ETHNICITY

As in the case of religion, difference of ethnicity tends to be destructive only if one partner feels a pride investment in his national background and his partner has another background. Nationalism as a high priority nearly always causes relating difficulties unless it is on both partners' priority list.

4. MONEY

Here again, money becomes a problem when interest in money is on only one partner's priority list. Incompatible priorities about money—a commodity our culture has endowed with great significance—can lead to frustration in terms of desired life-style and outlook generally.

5. PLEASURABLE PURSUITS
For some people the pursuit of pleasure is high on a list of priorities. For others it is of relatively low priority: they accept pleasure if it comes, but they don't "pursue it." This priority, too, can be a determinant of an individual's lifestyle, and can cause problems if one partner in a relationship pursues pleasure and the other does not.

6. TIME
To some people time—punctuality, the efficient use of time, scheduling—is truly of the essence: it is high on their list of priorities. To others it has no meaning at all: they are casual about appointments, noncompulsive about deadlines, and very often not as goal-oriented as people who count time as a high priority. Obviously these feelings reflect entirely different life-styles, and a divergence of priority here can be seriously disruptive to a relationship.

7. INTEGRITY
As I've explained elsewhere, particularly in our discussion of "issue-oriented" as opposed to "people-oriented" character types, integrity—the truth above all—does not have the same importance on everyone's list of priorities. Divergence about integrity need not be a disaster for a relationship if a live-and-let-live attitude prevails. But if one partner adheres to a principle-above-people dictum, differences in priorities can lead to major schisms.

8. PEOPLE
Differences of priorities regarding the importance of people in one's life can lead to major difficulties, as this deeply affects style of life. High priority in this area usually means spending

a good deal of time with people. Also, as I indicated earlier, a high people priority often means greater investment in loyalty to people than adherence to principle—which can mean a divergence of priorities about integrity.

9. FAMILY LIFE

Family life—involvements, attachments, social existence—has top priority for some people whose entire self-identifying springs from this source. On the other end of the scale are people to whom family life has little or no meaning and who sustain marked detachment from family ties of any kind. When there is a divergence of priorities about family life, both partners in a relationship may drift into detachment.

10. CHILDREN

Having children, emotional investment in children, involvement with children—these issues can be of great importance in determining how life is conducted among human beings. Major discrepancies in priorities here inevitably lead to gross dissatisfactions between partners, whether those partners are married or just socially friendly. (Think of all the couples who have stopped seeing former friends because the friends are "totally wrapped up in their children.") Having children does not remedy a sick relationship; but children as a mutually shared high priority may be a significant help for a faltering relationship.

11. ROMANCE

An existence without romance is unthinkable for some people. For others it is low on the priority scale—pragmatism is all. The place of romance in the hierarchy of priorities has great influence on style of life and may make compatible life-styles impossible if the divergence is too great.

12. EXCITEMENT AND PEACE

These function in the same way as romance. People who make excitement a high priority often view peace as lethargic paralysis. People who value peace often view excitement as manic chaos—a turbulent threat to well-being.

13. WORK

High-priority work people often see work as the center of their identity and life. Low-priority work people see it as a necessary nuisance that gets in the way of leisure activities. Of course, priority here affects life-style, tastes, proclivities, values, choices, decisions, and actions. This is a big one!

14. INTELLECTUAL ACTIVITY

Intellectual *interests*, which determine life-style as well as choice of social activity and confreres or social partners, are more important than the actual measure of intelligence.

15. PHYSICAL ACTIVITY

Discrepancies here may not be catastrophic: a couple, or two friends, may differ about the importance of exercise, sport, or simply getting out of the house. Much depends on the other priorities as well as the degree of live and let live.

Obviously there is much overlapping of crucial priorities. Also, each affects and is affected by all the others. Of course, in great mutual dependency, divergence in priorities offers much more difficulty than where greater health and individuality exist. Common priorities make it easier for two relating partners to understand each other—they make a *cooperative* relationship more possible. Divergent priorities make it necessary for both partners to struggle that much more for a common frame of reference and understanding. All things being equal, intimacy is also fostered by common priorities, simply because enjoying the same things brings people closer together.

Laurence and Sylvia

Business is his world. Art is hers. They are both very successful in terms of our culture. He is the chairman of the board of a major company and earns a great deal of money. Her paintings have appeared in prestigious galleries and also in several museums. They fetch high prices.

People ask what they have in common. The answer: an interest in the principle of "live and let live" and little else. Her interest in business is nil, and his interest in art is nil. They have lived apart together for over twenty years. And yet they help each other in their fashion. They have no children and little spare time. Her art and his business activities take up nearly all their waking time and energy. What spare time they do have is devoted to totally different pursuits. He likes sports. She likes museums. They do not share the same friends.

They do escort each other to large benefit affairs, which they go to on occasion. And they share their economic needs and responsibilities effectively. They are sexual partners, too, although their sexual activity is rather infrequent. On occasion through the years they have had brief affairs with other people. They each know this but don't talk about it, and there seems to be no great resentment on this score.

Why do they stay together? Indeed, why did they get married at all? Their relationship is in large part one of convenience. They are essentially conventional people. They like to dress well, live well, and they "look good together," Sylvia says. They both feel that marriage has given them considerably more prestige among their friends and has helped Laurence professionally. Sylvia also feels that it was something she needed to do eventually, so she "got it over with and tucked away."

They seem to have nothing in common, but what they do have is important to them. These are essentially alienated and detached people. They use each other to exercise their detachment. They need each other as people to keep a distance from and, in so doing, sustain the illusion of independence. Their marriage protects them from deeper commitments to other people. An occasional affair with someone else provides stimulation and sexual excitement—a kind of pseudo-aliveness—but its main function is probably to confirm a feeling of independence from each other. They probably suffer from a good deal of underlying loneliness and dependency. This is inevitable in people of limited emotional investment. A deep sense of isolation always prevails in these cases. Laurence is essentially monomaniacal about his business, and Sylvia is the same about her art. Their professions are used to tune out feelings generally, especially feelings of isolation.

It must be remembered that any hints of dependency, feelings of loneliness, the need for other people are anxiety-provoking to the very detached. Laurence and Sylvia use each other unconsciously to help ward off the anxiety that would be generated by consciousness of a need for others. They have worked out a way of life that permits enough cooperative living to give an image of conventional, social solidity, while it secretly dilutes loneliness and isolation. At the same time, it permits their major neurotic defenses against anxiety—alienation and detachment—to go on relatively undisturbed.

Marge and Cindy

Marge is fifty-five, widowed, and has a daughter almost Cindy's age. Cindy is thirty-five. Her own mother is sixty-five, ten years older than Marge. Cindy has had boyfriends but has never been married. The two women have known each other for ten years, having met at a college alumni function. Despite their difference in age, they found they had many common interests and priorities, and a longstanding, very close relationship developed. After a short time their age difference seemed to be a negligible factor that "didn't matter at all."

They each attend social functions involving the other's friends and are completely at ease with adults of all ages. The two women have helped each other in many ways over the years and have even proved to be self-sacrificing and thoroughly loyal during some very difficult periods. These involved money and health; neither stinted or held back when help was needed.

But when they are together they bicker and snap at each other almost constantly. At times they recite long lists of complaints and display considerable anger, sometimes so much so that one forgets that their relationship is essentially a cooperative one replete with kindness and trust. But although they may appear antagonistic, the underlying dynamic is cooperative, neither adversarial nor antagonistic. The fact that they share so many interests and priorities makes it possible for them to maintain a satisfying relationship.

In fact, their bickering has a quite different cause. Although Marge relates to Cindy with great openness and trust—as does Cindy to Marge—Marge has no such relationship with her daughter, and Cindy has no such relationship with her own mother. In the case of their own relatives, their idealized images and self-effacement block the possibility of open and nonduplicitous deep relating. The fact is, Marge sees herself as the ideal mother, Cindy sees herself as the ideal daughter. "Ideals" in both cases prevent honest expressions of dissatisfaction of any kind, let alone the admission or, even worse, the expression of anger. Their relationships with their closest relatives remain unsullied, unreal, and idealized, so as to preserve the particular idealized versions of self.

Marge does a great deal for her daughter, having come to her rescue in several crisis situations, and has given unstintingly of her time and energy. The same is true of Cindy and her mother. Cindy is utterly devoted and anticipates her mother's every need long before it is spoken. But these relationships remain largely superficial because they are idealized and unreal; thus, real feelings and emotional validity are not exchanged and remain stinted.

Marge and Cindy have a much deeper relationship, a much more open one, a relationship replete with real exchange of feelings. These women have considerable emotional investment in each other, unblocked by the need for self-idealization in any area.

Many of their complaints about each other are poorly founded and exaggerated. They are largely a form of psychodrama. Although they relate as equals and peers for the most part, they displace much feeling, especially repressed anger, to each other that they really feel for their relatives. Marge displaces her anger at her daughter to Cindy, and Cindy displaces anger at her mother to Marge. Their relationship can take it because it is essentially open and strong. It is not hampered, blocked, and made fragile by the need to be ideal. Indeed, it partly works in the service of idealization as applied to the relationships with their relatives and to self-idealization as perfect mother and perfect daughter. Interestingly, their own relationship seems to go on, relatively unscathed by its use in protecting their idealized relationships with blood relatives from reality.

IV

SOCIETY AND
CULTURE

CULTURAL IMPACT

We cannot exaggerate the impact of society and culture on how we relate. This is not to say that we are complete innocents victimized by cultural dicta over which we have no control. If we seem to behave like armies of self-destructive automatons, it is because we respond to society in neurotic ways, neglecting to struggle for individuality. In capitulating to societal pressures, we often refuse to tap our own human and healthy resources. Also, if society's customs are dictated by society itself— that is, the many millions of us—we are dictating the terms of our own surrender.

We are a competitive, hierarchical, success-oriented society, in which success is measured in terms of material wealth, power, prestige, notoriety, not of cooperation, peace, or health. And the destructive elements of society are transmitted to its basic relating units by the professional and business worlds, by schools of all kinds, by the media. However, the family itself is probably the most important vehicle for the transmission of cultural messages, for it is a microcosm of the culture. The family members each have their assigned role and hierarchical status. There are the "successes" and "failures"; the guilty and guilt-producers; the "poor" but highly manipulative "souls"; the respected and the persons of no standing; the "strong" and the "weak." None of this is lost on the child. It is all heavy propaganda and registers in the unconscious even when it is not fully appreciated consciously.

From my point of view, the most destructive messages to relationships delivered by our culture are important enough to discuss separately in the sections that follow. These messages encourage simplistic notions about the self, leading us to repress aspects of our character in a search for a "simple solution"; they encourage adversary and antagonistic relationships and demean cooperation.

ANGER

How we experience anger affects our emotional life and our relationships at least as much and perhaps more than is true of any other human emotion, and yet the cultural messages we receive about anger are decidedly mixed, producing confusion, internal conflict, anxiety, neurotic stratagems, and interpersonal difficulties. What is this mixed message? It is that we must be *nice*, we must be popular, we must be universally loved—and to be these things, we must not get angry or express anger. The expression of anger equals lack of control; "cool" people (especially macho men) do not get angry, or at least don't show anger even if they feel it. On the other hand, society tells us, self-assertive people both get angry and show anger. This is especially characteristic of strong macho men. The new woman is allowed to be angry. So anger equals strength, while, at the same time, anger equals potential murder.

Anger cannot be repressed without destructive repercussions. Emotional substitutes for appropriate expressions of anger—undue anxiety, psychosomatic symptoms like high blood pressure or asthmatic attacks, unreasonable fears, compulsions, depression, obesity, self-imposed starvation, insomnia, obsessiveness, and so on—are extremely destructive to oneself. A weakened self does not do well in relating to others. But there are also effects of repression that directly destroy the relating process itself.

Anger is often expressed as a mood. There is no verbalization, there isn't even a signal, such as sullen coldness; something much more subtle is expressed through the mood of the angry person. The mood may be projected by tone, by movement, by a subtle ignoring of other people's presence—passing by them as if they are not there, interrupting when they talk. It is often so subtle that the other person doesn't know consciously that it exists. But he or she responds to it by feeling rejected and responding accordingly with hurt feelings and anger, which are difficult to express because they seem inappropriate. This is so because there is no conscious aware-ness of the other person's angry mood.

Repressed anger is often converted to anger at oneself, which becomes self-hate. The anger must go *somewhere*, and when other outlets are considered socially unacceptable, the only target left is oneself. The result is an implosion rather than an explosion. Self-hate takes many forms: depression, self-recrimination, and every conceivable kind of self-sabotage, including the formation of de-structive relationships. Obviously a sick, self-hating person is not the best relating partner. But self-hate often is also unconsciously projected onto one's partner, who is then viewed with loathing. Additionally, any aspect of the partner that is seen as the same or similar to one's own hated characteristics is despised. People who project their anger and self-hate in this way often tend also to displace anger at or from other sources to loved ones. Anger at bosses, teachers, and colleagues, or at personal failure and uncon-trollable circumstances, is unconsciously displaced to close part-ners, especially ones who can be trusted not to retaliate. Projections often take place between two partners who are convinced of the validity and appropriateness of their displaced anger. But since the *real* sources of rage remain unconscious and untouched, the anger never subsides and they are left feeling destructively antagonistic to each other.

Anger is often displaced to the sexual area, turning it into a combative arena. Repressed anger often leads to sexual anesthesia, in which the individual cannot feel or be stimulated. It produces personal and mutual frustration—sometimes preceded by teasing and potential promise. It is often expressed through sexual dysfunctions, including premature ejaculation, lack of interest, impotence, and inability to achieve orgasm. It may also be represented by personal neglect—uncleanliness, sloppy dressing, obesity—whose object is to make oneself less attractive. It may be expressed through chronic flirting and compulsive promiscuity. The anger generating these symptoms or symbols or expressions may involve the sexual partner directly, may be displaced from other people, or may be both, but is seldom felt as anger. To make things better, the individuals involved must become aware of it as anger and get at its sources or generating roots.

Often repressed anger is experienced eventually in vindictive explosive outbursts. These may vary from minor temper tantrums to severe hysterical manifestations (such as pseudo-convulsive seizures, amnesia, physical paralysis, blindness) to self-destructive physical illnesses (such as heart attacks) or to acts like suicide and murder.

Contrary to popular opinion, the *appropriate* expression of anger has no such deleterious effects. It is almost invariably that "nice, quiet," utterly blank, seemingly affectless person whose eventual explosive outbursts of accumulated wrath produce uncontrollable violence. There are inappropriate and hurtful ways of expressing storehouses of repressed anger: even relatively mild explosions are not conducive to happy relating. They produce fear in both partners as well as in bystanders such as children. They usually add to confusion, and the effects are so unpleasant that honest expressions of anger are even further inhibited. This in turn increases repression and contributes to further explosions—and a vicious circle is established. Explosions of anger, especially massive and chronic ones, usually result in complete communication breakdown and related disintegration and dissolution.

Gossip is a destructive form of expressing anger and makes for extremely disturbed relationships. Hostile remarks, distortions, exaggerations, and lies are insinuated; direct confrontation with principals involved is avoided. Gossip, in addition to being a sneaky way to discharge anger, is also often used to entertain: you give out spurious information in an effort to win admiration or to be liked. Its use for either or both purposes remains essentially out of conscious awareness of the user. Gossip has an addictive quality, and habitual use of it can become increasingly malignant, affecting the gossip's friend and foe alike.

Another way of expressing anger is to employ various kinds of subtle sabotage. These may include compulsive lateness, demoralizing and overtly hostile remarks, giving misleading information or poor advice. The corrosive effect of this mechanism on the relating process is obvious. It is also possible for anger to wear a mask of honesty: some of the most devastating vindictive attacks can be justified on the basis of so-called honesty. The same is true of gossip in which the information conveyed may be factual. Motivation is obviously of great importance in this connection. Truth can be used in the service of inflicting great emotional pain and cruelty.

Sullenness mixed with withdrawal—the production and extension of an emotional vacuum—is one of the most destructive expressions of anger in human relationships. This mechanism guarantees a breakdown in communication and fosters a hostility that has no effective outlet or expression. An emotional pall settles on a household in which this mechanism is used and adversely affects all members, including innocent young children. Quite often, breaks in the vacuum take place only in the form of destructive, explosive outbursts, and fear of these outbursts can make withdrawal more insidious, intense, and chronic. This particular mechanism is often used as a sadistic ploy—withholding emotional contact from a partner who is sorely in need of it, and often desperately dependent on contact, even in the form of abrasive friction. Any contact, even a painful one, is preferable to the dependent partner: pleas to "vilify me, even hit me, but don't shut me out" are a response to the intense pain of being cut off and cut out emotionally. Obviously, this mechanism delivers the message of anger, but it does so in an extremely destructive way. The message is not clear or clean. The reasons for anger are seldom clarified, if expressed at all, and the air is never cleared. The wrath stays inside, festers, grows, and has its malignant effect on all concerned. Sullen coldness is an ideal vehicle for vindictiveness—which is ultimately always destructive to relationships.

Anger cannot be repressed without the repression of other feelings, too. The human psyche is simply not that selective. When we repress anger, we deaden our feelings. Anger, unfelt and unexpressed, sits as a block to other emotions, most importantly feelings of love, tenderness, openness, intimacy. These are freed only when the block of anger is removed. Vitalizing angry feelings frees and vitalizes feelings of love. This alienating and blocking effect is perhaps the most destructive aspect of repressing anger in terms of relating.

Exchanging feelings constitutes relating. In antagonistic relationships, anger is used in the service of vindictive triumph. In adversary relationships, it is used to generate energy for self-assertion. In cooperative relationships, anger is used to convey real feelings of displeasure. As feeling human beings we must at times feel angry, and to express that emotion openly and warmly—at the time it occurs and to the person who occasions it—is the only way to real friendship. No matter what society tells us about anger, its expression permits clearing the air, reconciling differences, and freeing the flow of all feelings needed for a rich relationship.

Perry and Sally

He complained of her "periodic attacks of coldness." "She just shuts off, as if there's nothing there—I just don't exist, and for that matter, she doesn't either. Lasts for weeks, even months—she says she just can't help it. Other times she's warm, close; the gentlest, sweetest person I know. Everyone loves Sally. And then, just like that—she goes through all the motions, you understand, but it's all mechanical, perfunctory, cold, and distant. To tell the truth, it turns me off—I've been seriously thinking of just getting out, walking off myself. I've had it.

"Yes, I've asked her about it again and again. *Ask* isn't really the word. I've confronted her; I've complained. Frankly, I've been close to tears a number of times. I just can't stand it. She never gets angry when I confront her. She says she's sorry, truly sorry, and I'm sure she is. She's really a nice person—a wonderful person. She says she just can't do anything about it. She feels that way, and she just can't turn off her feelings. I bought her a present for her birthday—she seemed appreciative, but not enthusiastic at all. Sex is the same way. She responds, but she's not really there, and I feel lost. You see, she's honest, she feels what she feels and she won't fake it or playact. I give her credit for that. But I sure miss honest-to-God affection."

I know him. I don't know her except through him. Here is my educated speculation as to what has been happening.

Sally and Perry are overtly both compliant and detached, with a hidden trend of expansiveness. Sally is more detached and Perry is more dependent. In their relationship, each is detached from the other, and each wants something different from the relationship: Sally needs more space and distance, though plenty of affection; Perry needs closeness.

"Sally never gets angry"—that has much significance. Like all people, Sally does, in fact, get angry from time to time. But she not only fails to demonstrate anger, she is alienated from it—she isn't aware, or doesn't want to be aware, of any angry feelings. She so quickly converts hot anger to coldness that she herself does not experience her anger. This is probably due to a long history of a compelling need to be liked and fear that anger will destroy her image and her lovability. Her coldness serves to camouflage her feelings and at the same time to express them, albeit in perverted form.

But her coldness greatly disturbs Perry; indeed, it punishes him—and she realizes this, though perhaps only on an unconscious

level. Knowing Perry, I suspect that his morbid dependent neediness is abrasive to her, and is especially grating to her need for
detachment, as well as coming into conflict with her own dependency.

Perry, of course, feels deprived and punished, and reacts by
thinking in terms of vindictiveness and detachment. He will become cold too, he thinks. Better yet, he will leave.

I suggested to Perry that he help Sally with her anger. He
should suggest to her the possibility of her being angry. If she resists
this concept, he should help to analyze this resistance by helping
her to understand her fear and inhibition in this regard. He must
reassure her of her lovability, indicating that warm anger is preferable to coldness and deadening of feelings. He must also struggle
to reduce his own neediness and to try to give her more of her own
space.

Sally must learn to help him with his dependency—instead of
"turning off," she must enter into dialogue with him regarding his
extraordinary neediness and fear of abandonment. They must exercise much compassion for themselves and for each other's difficulties, and above all must stop reacting to each other's neurotic
stratagems. This may be possible only if both undertake a course of
analytic treatment. In analytic treatment a critical goal would be
to expose and to reduce the intensity of all the trends. In so doing,
mutual dependency would be reduced in terms of expecting each
other to live out hidden needs—in this case, expansiveness—thus
ultimately reducing unconscious claims on each other and neu-
tralizing anger.

Lilly and Abe

She complains about him all the time. (He's annoyed but doesn't
say much.) Somehow everything is his fault. Any difficulties with
the house, money, family, vacations—it's all his fault. Problems she
has, as with making decisions or feeling bored or lonely or depressed
or anxious, are always traced to Abe. If he'd only change, she says,

everything would be okay, but "talking to him is like talking to a stone wall." She's particularly angry at him because he keeps going to business, playing golf, going out with friends, and "laughing it up," even though she's miserable so much of the time and he's the cause of it. He is also, she is certain, responsible for their largely unsatisfactory sex life.

He says, when asked, that he just doesn't understand her complaints or her moods or her recriminations against him. "Am I supposed to give up golf and everything else that relaxes me to make her happy? Would she be better off if I was miserable too? She goes out to buy a dress and gets into a stew because she can't make up her mind. I go out to buy a suit, and I buy one. Then she's enraged with me. Somehow she turns things around so that it's my fault she can't buy a dress." He shrugs his shoulders and goes on with things the way they are.

Though Lilly can get pretty vindictive, and Abe's silences and refusal to joust with her are a considerable weapon in his arsenal, they don't really fit the dynamics of an antagonistic relationship. In fact, they don't really reject each other. But they don't fit readily into any other category either. I believe that an inability to define a relationship with any one of the paradigms we've discussed is often an indication that we are dealing with more than usual disturbance. In time, I found that this is the case with Lilly and Abe.

Lilly, it turned out, suffers from severe and paralyzing mood swings fed by intense self-hate. Abe suffers from considerable alienation and detachment, as well as from intense self-hate. If they represent a lock, she fluctuates from identification with expansive narcissism to severe self-effacement (coupled with extreme morbid dependency and compliance). He represents detachment. The usual characteristic of sadomasochistic jousting with periodic role changing is not in evidence, so one cannot say they have a basic sadomasochistic relationship.

In a way though, on a deeper than usual level, they participate in a kind of cooperative relationship—neurotic though it is. The major dynamic force of the relating process here is a chronic and severe exchange of blame. Without it suicide might be a possibility.

Yes, they use each other to project their self-hate and to relieve themselves. Lilly projects her anger at herself onto Abe, blaming him for all her personal inadequacies. Abe substitutes Lilly's tirades for the attacks he would otherwise make on himself. And he rationalizes this use of Lilly as aggressor by saying, "What am I supposed to do? Like living with a saber-toothed tiger. Have to shut her out to protect myself."

These people talk about leaving each other. But they don't. The central glue here is anger and its externalization. Deep down, they know that without it they would have to confront raging self-hate. Could healthier relating take place? Yes, but the possibility of a different kind of relating is based on true expression of anger and reduction of self-hate. This, as I've indicated, involves a confrontation with self-hate on a fully conscious basis, and this presents great risk. Self-hate can be reduced only after a heroic struggle to change one's perfectionistic, idealized image of oneself and the human condition.

The development of compassion for self and others is not easy. Learning what it is to be a real, imperfect person in the real world is an ongoing, never-ending struggle. Should these people embark on this struggle, all kinds of possibilities would present themselves. They may relate more healthily to each other, or they may find that they prefer to part after all and to embark on other relationships.

Without the need for, or the binding quality of, an intense, ongoing externalizing process, all kinds of possibilities come into existence. But these are also not without risk. Disturbed people know this deep down and also are aware of their vulnerability and fragility. Most often they prefer the familiarity of sick relating, however destructive, to the possibility of healthier but unfamiliar and risky new ways and/or partners.

IDEALIZATIONS AND DISTORTIONS ABOUT LOVE AND SEX

We are told again and again, in songs, novels, movies, television, and by professionals, too—people who work as therapists—that love can conquer all, that it is a cure for what ails us. The love they speak of is, I'm afraid, a highly idealized version, and believing in this or a number of other false truisms about love can pollute all our relating efforts.

Togetherness: Our culture exalts a kind of malignant, two-headed monster of togetherness, even as it extols the manly virtues of macho apartness. We are told that love is utterly binding, and come to believe that our love is equated with wanting to be together always, to enjoy the same things, people, interests, and activities at the same time. We are told we must always prefer each other's company to anyone else's. This invariably makes for feelings of being crowded, burdened, enslaved, and tyrannized by one's partner in love—the very essence of being *locked in*.

A belief in perfect togetherness extends into the sexual area and generates the quest for a nonexistent perfect sexual harmony, in which tastes, appetites, and timing are always synchronized. This, of course, results in disappointment, anger, depression, continued questing, and frustration in lieu of mutual accommodation.

Nonverbal communication: Many people in our society have somehow come to believe that minimal word messages are necessary between people in love. This is especially seen in sexual activity, where the need to state preferences is interpreted as an indication of less than perfect loving and sexual harmony. The idea "If I have to tell you, the whole thing is spoiled" really means that love obliterates the need for verbal communication. This is part of the general mystique of love fostered by society, in highly romanticized notions, through song and drama, of the supernatural powers inherent in being on the same loving wavelength.

But few if any of us have the power of mental telepathy. Love of people and between people involves the need to understand and to be understood. This entails the use of language, through which mutual communication grows only with practice. In a relationship that relies dogmatically on telepathic communication, whole sets of expectations will grow up in the mind of one partner of which the other partner is not aware. This leads inevitably to frustration and anger, pushing the partners toward an antagonistic relationship. It takes experience, mutual experience in speaking and listening, to understand what words and symbols really mean to each of us, let alone to build a common language characteristic of a creative relationship.

Jealousy: While promoted as a certain sign of the "real thing," in fact, jealousy is a destroyer of fruitful relating and is not at all a function of love. Chronic jealousy springs from poor self-esteem and pathological insecurity, in which the individual feels that anyone else is preferable to him or her. Acute jealous attacks are almost invariably due to hurt pride and to immediate blows to self-esteem. These often can be traced to lost jobs, rejections, examination failures, or other seeming or actual personal assaults. Jealousy undermines the trust necessary for cooperative relating.

Possessiveness: Jealousy is often linked to morbid possessiveness, which is extremely abrasive and stressful to the relating process. Possessiveness is also often confused with love. It invariably has the same or similar dynamics to those of jealousy and has no connection to anything that may be construed as mature love.

Possessiveness is often the function of morbid dependency as well as of extreme narcissism, and can be frequently found in relationships characterized by sadomasochism. Possessiveness is characteristic of people whose emotional development was arrested at an infantile level; it often takes the form of claims: "If you really love me, you will give me what I need"; "If you love me, you will never get angry at me" (of course, anger and love are not at all mutually exclusive); "You will always understand and help me even if it means sacrificing your own values"; "You will enjoy what I enjoy"; "If you loved me, you would never disagree—never get angry"; "I cannot live without you"; "If you loved me, you would not have stopped buying me things"; "If you loved me, you would be with me always, no matter what." Possessiveness has a constricting effect on a relationship—it sets conditions on the partnership and leads to adversarial feelings.

Exclusivity: Exclusivity in this context equals both love and personal prestige. Exclusivity here means singular interest in each other, singular attraction to each other, and singular feelings, especially sexual feelings, about each other, to the exclusion of even possibility of interest, attraction, or feelings toward anyone else. Love in this context is idealized so as to remove the possibility of temptations of any kind that involve other people. It also precludes interests of any kind that may conceivably detract from complete preoccupation with each other.

However much human beings are lovingly involved, we are simply not constructed to have feelings only for a loved one. Regardless of how we choose to behave relative to our feelings, yearnings, and temptations, we will experience feelings, if nothing else, relative to different people at least part of the time. Thus, the demand for exclusivity produces repression, anxiety, self-hate, and depression. Purity simply is not a human characteristic.

Love as a Solution, or "Love Conquers All"

Love does *not*—contrary to myth—cure all diseases, solve economic ills, provide perfect communication, dispel sexual problems, dilute and counteract ignorance and prejudice, remove temptations, resolve internal and external conflicts, produce bliss, or serve as an ever-effective anti-anxiety agent and antidepressant. Love—real love, the kind characterized by kindness, caring, respect for mutual sensibilities and proclivities, openness, trust, tenderness, and intimacy—may help make problems bearable or solvable. But its effect is limited. It is not a panacea. Indeed, even the most loving people, as well as people deeply infatuated with each other, must still struggle to understand the other's sensibilities, values, and yearnings. This is especially true of people who don't even know their own minds, so to speak. Very often the claim on love is for the lover to instantly perceive inner frustrations and difficulties and make them go away. People who expect love to be a cure-all often feel that each problem that arises in their life and that is not instantly resolved is evidence of a failure in a loving relationship. This of course produces often irreparable damage.

Infatuation and love: We are inundated with the message that the heightened feelings and great excitement characteristic of infatuations or crushes is the "real thing." This is not surprising in a society largely given to stimulation addiction. But unfortunately we come to believe that these feelings must be sustained throughout deep, prolonged relationships. Of course these feelings are characteristic of new relationships with unfamiliar people—they come from the excitement of being newly accepted or of making new conquests. But this belief in excitement as proof of valid love is destructive to sustained relationships, which are interpreted as lacking love when initial excitement wanes. So the partners split up, seeking to recapture the thrill with unfamiliar people; the result is short, aborted relationships, unrequited yearnings, and general disappointment.

In a morbidly dependent relationship we sometimes see hero worship and infatuation sustained for a lifetime. Masochists cling to infatuation with a "strong" partner, because melding with that partner seems a way to have strength, too. Of course, such infatuations obliterate one's real self and make true self-development impossible; they also affect the partner on whom all kinds of idealistic claims are made for nonexistent perfection.

The most significant aspect of infatuation is the lack of caring for the other person as a real person, rather than as an aberrated image. In what we may call real loving relationships, there is real caring about real people. In infatuations, time and energy are spent largely in the service of idealization. We project idealized versions of ourselves onto other people and then become infatuated with those idealizations. We also become infatuated with people to whom we can displace characteristics we were impressed with in other people from early times in our lives—especially parents. Additionally, we tend to form crushes on people who seem to be prototypes of culturally accepted images, especially with regard to superficialities such as their material possessions, notoriety, and looks. We also become infatuated with people with whom we can impress other people. Not that we are aware that we are doing this; on the contrary, we pretend to ourselves that our feelings represent a real commitment to the other person. As this very subtle and insidious effect of obsessive infatuation develops, it "protects" the individual in question from real and adult commitment and involvement, even as it fools the person into believing he is totally and obsessively involved.

Real relating involves real people, real sustained involvement and closeness, real exchanges of all kinds, real knowledge of each other's values, needs, desires, and *real human limitations*. It involves *real caring*. Infatuations, on the other hand, are essentially make-believe relationships. Crushes are often experienced at a distance and usually involve only one person, a supplicant. Sometimes the idealized person is not actually known at all by the supplicant, and remains unaware of the supplicant's feelings. The crush involves extension of self through the glorification of the individual of whom we are obsessed. As such, it is a form of narcissism. Mature relating involves seeing the other individual as separate and whole, with all the limitations inherent in being human. It also involves individual needs, often not our own, for which we have respect. This respect for others' needs is almost always the antithesis of the claims of infatuation.

Jenny and Bob

She met him once. After that she saw him a number of times. She doesn't believe he saw her again. After their initial meeting she never spoke to him again. When they met—at a mutual friend's house—they spoke for twenty minutes. It was all small talk; they hardly spoke about themselves. "He didn't take my number or flirt in any way. After all, he's married," says Jenny. "He certainly impressed me."

In subsequent months she found out a lot about him through people they knew in common. She would stand outside his office, his apartment house, his paddle-tennis club, or eat in a restaurant one table away from him, in order to see him. He never noticed her, and she never approached him. She is thirty-two. He is thirty-eight. As she said, he is married. She is not. She does go out on dates, but she never stops thinking about him. All the men she meets "pale by comparison." He is everything she ever dreamed of.

She knows a lot of facts about him, and yet she doesn't know him at all—"not really," she says. She keeps it that way. Though she is fairly aggressive and has approached a number of men many times, she says she would never approach him. "Besides, he is married," she insists. She never stops thinking or daydreaming about him. "He is my whole life. People would think I'm crazy if they knew. Saw him making a phone call in a booth near his house a week ago. The way he moves and talks—I get palpitations." This obsession has been going on for three and a half years.

Jenny's essential dependency is hidden by an outer veneer of aggressiveness that enables her to manipulate social situations to a small extent. But underneath she yearns for an idealized knight in shining armor, a dream that goes back to early childhood fantasies that compensated for a weak, self-effacing father. What she actually knows of the real Bob through observation and investigation fits her early fantasy extremely well. Her imagination has filled in the rest.

Bob's unavailability is crucial. It protects the image from any flaws that would inevitably come to light if real confrontation took place. She keeps this idealized image of a man pure and untarnished by reality. In so doing, she can also enjoy martyred self-glorification through romantic suffering from unrequited love for the godlike unattainable. By now Bob has indeed become godlike: she, a mere mortal, can only worship at a distance, being much too lowly to contemplate a real liaison of any kind.

An obsessive infatuation like this destroys the possibility of Jenny's relating to other men on a serious basis because they "pale by comparison." Indeed, her preoccupation with Bob serves as a diversion from nearly all Jenny's problems, and she avoids life generally through this mechanism. She also reinforces her self-effacement by casting herself in the role of helpless lady supplicant.

Jenny knows that she needs help "in order to start really living." She realizes that she doesn't know Bob at all. She is not psychotic. She says realistically that she is certain he doesn't know she exists. But she also says, "I hate to give him up. I have no one else." Getting anyone else on these terms—to fit the idealized characteristics attributed to Bob—will be impossible. A desperate struggle to surrender fantasy and inhuman standards must take place; otherwise Jenny's relating life will be disappointing at best and empty at worst.

Sexual Misinformation

The stress our society places on being sexually attractive, on sexual performance, on conquest, on achievement of orgasm—cataclysmic, multiple, prolonged, or vaginal—pressures sexual partners, disappoints them, creates anxiety and feelings of inadequacy, and causes each partner to make claims on the other or to displace and project self-hate.

A complicating polarization of expectations has arisen in recent years: On the one hand, a unisexual, androgynous outlook sees men and women as being exactly alike in desire, needs, and responses. At the other pole, they are seen as being totally different and therefore with no capacity to understand each other's proclivities, needs, or responses. Neither extreme is true, of course! Men and women are the same in terms of need and desire for satisfaction, but there are obvious physiological differences between them, and the range of possibility in terms of desire, preference, and response is enormous for both sexes.

The mechanics of sex have been sold and resold by a society more interested in concrete superficialities than in feelings and relationships as symbolized and expressed through sex. Any marriage manual will tell you what you want to know—there isn't that much to it. But this stress on mechanics is destructive. It leads to superficialities and to pride investment in performance rather than to healthy interest in richer relating. Sexual athletics simply do not provide long-lasting or deeper satisfactions, and to expect them to do so is asking for disappointment—disappointment that is destructive to all areas of the relationship.

Another area where sexual propaganda can sabotage relationships is that of masturbation. Masturbation is interpreted as hostile to the opposite sex (and therefore as potentially homosexual); as evidence of lack of mature control; as masculine; as okay for unmarried men or women; and as a sign of sexual discord or failing attraction in married couples. Mutual masturbation is seen as less than the "real thing" and therefore as bad. Masturbation is viewed as characteristic of adolescence and evidence of retarded sexual and even emotional development in adults. All this leads the individual who masturbates into feelings of inadequacy and self-hate, and causes mutual recriminations, claims, and disturbances in any relationship. "If you love me, how come you do that—couldn't you wait?" says the other partner. "Aren't I attractive enough?" And so on. Masturbation and mutual stimulation are common practices in both sexes at all ages, whether the individuals live alone or together. It can be used to relieve sexual tension, especially since people are arrhythmic and one partner may not feel sexually stimulated at a time when the other does. Sometimes, used as an adjunct, masturbation may be more effective than intercourse alone in attaining satisfaction.

The importance of orgasm is overstressed by our society. Not everyone needs or wants orgasms all the time in sexual activity. For many people, feelings of closeness—expressed sexually with and without orgasm—are of primary importance. But much cultural propaganda deprecates sex that does not culminate in mutual orgasm as well as sex in which orgasm is achieved through means other than intercourse.

In many quarters, sexual malfunction is viewed as a primary problem. I feel it may well *aggravate* primary problems, but the primary problem in any sexual dysfunction is usually based on general relating difficulties. To blame an unhealthy relationship on unsatisfying sex is to ignore the real problems.

In our society much is made of monogamous and "faithful" relationships: sexual contact with someone other than one's partner or mate is called infidelity, and it is unfailingly considered evidence of lack of love, of lack of interest, of irresponsibility, of "cheating." Any or all of these things may be true, or they may have no validity whatsoever. Nevertheless, I think these beliefs themselves can actually cause unwanted breakup and divorce as a result of peer pressure and hurt pride (pride in being the object of exclusive sexual interest to one's partner). "Infidelity" may also be due to anxiety, depression, feelings of inadequacy, repressed rage, childish curiosity, the inability to say no to self and to others, poor frustration tolerance, and inadequate sexual adjustment between partners, or any number of things. Love does not guarantee exclusivity of sexual interest. People are attracted to all kinds of people constantly, regardless of whether or not they love a particular person. What they *do* about the attraction is determined largely by past personal history, what they have been taught to do, and personal values, compulsions, and choices. "Fidelity" or "infidelity" can't—in and of itself—change a relationship.

These kinds of sexual misinformation are destructive to the sexual health of any relationship and lead to dissatisfaction and disturbance between would-be relating lovers. Undue emphasis on concrete, mechanical expertise; performance anxiety; stereotyping of "ideal" lovers, as well as of "ideal" response; all these have diluted the connection between sex and affection. To say no when we mean yes, to play games involving false resistance, teasing, confused messages, affectations of all kinds can be very destructive and often turn into sadomasochistic sexual warfare. While this may produce temporary excitement, it may also destroy feelings of tenderness and warmth. Prudery and false modesty have a destructive effect on spontaneity and can eventually lead to extreme frustration and lack of interest.

Gender Identification Confusion

Our society is replete with mixed and confusing messages about what constitutes masculinity and femininity. To make things more confusing, the messages keep changing, often in response to advertisers. According to current television commercials, women sweat less than men; women—real, attractive, sexy women—are thin, flat-chested, and invariably long-legged. They also are haughty to the point of disdain and contempt. Men have chiseled features, smoke, are wild about sports, often irrational, and love to munch junk foods, like squirrels, while watching television. Men are concerned with status positions and economics, while women are fascinated by the differences between eye makeups and detergents. Occasionally they are equally concerned about "ring around the collar," though even on this heady issue their concerns are expressed in different ways.

But more important messages are delivered subtly; they played insidious roles in our culture long before the advent of television, radio, and advertising. In any case, the various confusions involving definitions of sexual or gender identification roles delivered by society are not lost on children. From the moment we are born we see them exhibited by mothers, fathers, and other siblings, and in the family members' interactions.

Men are "stronger" than women. Strength in this connection is seen as rigidity, stubbornness, and often mild to moderate sadism. Many women have been brainwashed from early in their lives to be attracted to this kind of "strong" man and equate him with a high degree of ability and responsibility. This is especially true of severely dependent, passive women.

Men should be leaders at home and manage finances.

Passivity is equated with femininity.

Feelings are feminine, and lack of feelings is a masculine attribute.

Logical thinking is masculine. Intuition is feminine.

Care of children and family and housework are feminine and instinctual rather than motivationally learned.

Men have greater sexual needs than women.

Women are more possessive, jealous, envious, and romantic. But strong men are jealous.

Interest in art, poetry, literature is feminine. Interest in sports and business is masculine.

Men prefer the company of men, while women prefer the company of women.

Women have a preference for deep relationships; men prefer shallow relationships.

Tenderness and intimacy are feminine characteristics.

Openness and trust are masculine characteristics.

Mastery, control, sadism, detachment, gregariousness, and silence are masculine attributes.

Self-effacement, compliancy, morbid dependency, narcissism, masochism, manipulative skills are feminine characteristics.

Gossip and wiliness are feminine, while being straightforward and honest is masculine.

Men are more competitive.

Aggression is masculine.

Understanding money is masculine.

Understanding children is feminine.

Dancing is feminine.

Speaking French is feminine.

Tennis is both masculine and feminine.

Men and women are deprived of self-realization in experiencing and developing all of their feelings because they fear being thought feminine (if they are men) or masculine (if they are women). They are relating as images of what they ought to be, rather than what they really are. They must take constant care not to expose their own "masculine" (if they are women) or "feminine" (if they are men) characteristics. This produces inhibition, constriction, and boredom. It is a form of role-playing affectation, the enemy of spontaneous exchange. Without the ability to be in touch with our full gamut of feelings—so-called masculine, feminine, and otherwise; feelings actually have no gender—we relate as fractions of ourselves. Relationships between alienated people are marked by impoverishment, duplicity, affectation, mutual hatred, neurotic strategies, and gross misunderstandings.

Phil and Maggie

Phil was a surgeon and Maggie was his wife. She was very proud of him, and for a long time he'd come home and describe his operations to her. She almost felt she was there in the operating room with him and sometimes actually described surgical procedures to friends of theirs. Some of them began to resent Maggie because she constantly bragged about Phil and his great surgical accomplishments. He was the specialist personified—indeed, little in life interested him outside of surgery. But for a long time this was all right for both of them. She took care of their home and two children. He had his work, and he served as her alter ego. In exchange, she was his chief booster.

But then the kids went off to college. They came home less and less frequently. Maggie was bored. Even surgery bored her. Her once-idealized Phil seemed "narrow and constricted." "He doesn't even miss the kids—his routine hasn't changed a bit," she complained. She became increasingly moody, even depressed. She no longer talked surgery or boasted about Phil's accomplishments.

Maggie decided to see a therapist. She was surprised to learn what her real feelings about Phil were. For several months the "real truth" came out. He was "childish, stunted, self-centered, and really dull." He hadn't grown at all. He was a "real infant," and she "suspected" he was also "a terrible male chauvinist." She had "wasted" her life on him. She also suspected that he was only a mediocre surgeon. He had never become chief of surgery or invented any new techniques. He never wrote any papers. She said he had published one paper, but that was years ago, and now she knew it was of minor consequence.

Things changed socially, too. Now, instead of being his main booster, she became his chief detractor. In any controversial discussion she always took the opposite side. Not because she was angry at him, she said, but because his views were always "so narrow" and "invariably wrong." She came to realize that he was "opinionated, dogmatic, and thought he knew it all just because he was a surgeon." She couldn't believe it. She must have been sleepwalking. How in the world had she ever married "this boorish, self-important, infantile person?"

Maggie had been playing the ideal "feminine" role in life, ignoring her *own* needs for self-assertion. Her father had been a pharmacist. He always wanted to be a doctor, but he didn't have the money. She loved her father dearly. She now knew that he was everything her husband was not. He was kind, considerate, and open-minded. He also loved to read—Phil never opened a book, other than a medical journal. She had "never thought of going to medical school myself." "Girls didn't in those days." She went to "a good college" and majored in philosophy. In her senior year, a friend introduced her to Phil. He had already started his residency in surgery. When her parents heard about him, they were very impressed. She was too, and they married while he was still in training, the same day she graduated from college. Most of his fellow residents were at the wedding. "Something like a West Point wedding—stethoscopes instead of swords. My parents were ecstatic, especially my father. It was all very romantic. I now realize that I didn't know Phil at all."

She still did not know Phil and showed no inclination to give herself the time to get to know him. He had provided a "masculine" vessel for both her father and herself to live through vicariously. But Maggie also transferred her feelings for her father to Phil. This included her idealization (a projection of her own self-idealization as well as her image of her father) and her rage and condemnation when she grew up to realize that both she and her father had fallen short of the mark. Phil was the fall guy for her anger and disappointment—anger at herself (she couldn't be a doctor and please her father because she was a girl) and anger at her father (by marrying her off to a man she didn't even know, she felt, he was trying to make up for not being a doctor himself). She also secretly felt that her father was the true male chauvinist because had she been a boy she would surely have been encouraged to go to medical school herself.

Her anger galvanized her, and—in her bitterness over the gender typecasting she felt she was a victim of—she decided she must take action at once. She totally resisted suggestions to wait. She refused to consider that she might be displacing feelings about her father to Phil, and she ignored insights involving transference, externalization, image building and smashing, or vicarious living. Mostly she resisted revelation of anger at her father. Disturbing her pure image of him was intolerable. She preferred to let Phil bear the brunt of all her anger.

Once she had mobilized and expressed her anger, her depression, which had never been that deep or strong, disappeared. She insisted, despite strong advice otherwise, on leaving treatment. She planned to divorce Phil and to get a Ph.D. in clinical psychology.

The "Ever After" Illusion

Marriage in our society is often seen as the beginning of a life of utter fulfillment—the dream finally come true—a perpetuity of the wedding celebration itself. Many people feel that finding the right mate will automatically lead to fulfillment on every level, to satisfaction of all needs, emotional, economic, social, and personal. Many see this new stage in their life as one that will make up for previous years of loneliness, lack of recognition, lack of self-realization; it is a kind of personal vindication, and even a vindictive triumph.

This illusion, fed by society, takes especially strong root in morbidly dependent people, who are particularly vulnerable to these would-be promises and who inevitably suffer the consequences of severe disappointment. It is, after all, the dream of the self-hating, self-effacing, dependent person to mate with and to be lost in a more perfect self, and through that self to vicariously live and experience life as a new, adequate person. This emotional meld takes place in marriage, and the claims made on that marriage and the partner are huge indeed. They are, in fact, a magnification of the expectation of happiness on every level forever and ever. The disappointment, self-hate, recrimination, rage, abused reactions, and sense of martyrdom that ensue run rampant in our population.

More often than not, when the illusion proves to be a catastrophic disappointment, it is not abandoned. Indeed, it is sustained with new vigor. "Other people are more lucky." "Just picked the wrong partner." These are common statements in this connection. These people, especially morbid dependent people, go on dreaming and yearning and believing that the myth is true and that it is only a question of finding the right partner. "Mr. Right," as he often is referred to in our society, really means "Mr. Perfect," who will make the dream of living happily ever after come true.

STIMULATION ADDICTION

Our population has inadvertently and unconsciously become addicted to stimulation—from noise, entertainment, news, gossip, every conceivable kind of activity. And as our need for still more excitement grows, our demands for heightened stimuli increase, even as our reactions are shorter-lived and our sensibilities become dulled. Boredom is the most common fear of the stimulation addict, and boredom is the thing that most often makes such a person unable to sustain a relationship with anyone else. "So-and-so bored me, and so we don't see each other anymore," says one of my patients.

But it is incorrect to say that some people bore us. We are bored because we refuse to reach into ourselves in relating to them. Since a stimulation addict seeks his addictive substance outside himself, his inner resources remain untapped and underdeveloped; they become less and less accessible. If he is involved in a relationship, he blames his partner for his boredom and deadness—he feels it's his partner's job to relieve his unhappiness. Since the problem is an internal one, no external solution exists, and his partner can-

not provide relief. The victim of boredom then seeks other partners, convinced that the problem simply lies in being in the wrong
relationship. This is, of course, a continuation of an externalizing
process, and it shows how the cultural addiction to stimulation
affects our relationships.

Sustained, deep relating has its exhilarating moments, but in
its day-to-day business it does not provide the constant stimulation
necessary for the addict. Cooperative relating does not lend itself
to high stimulation. Stimulation addicts, especially those of the
chronic variety, tend toward antagonistic, sadomasochistic relationships. Cooperative and even adversary relating do not usually
satisfy the needs of the addict. Indeed, even long-standing sadomasochistic and antagonistic relating usually wear thin.

In response to frustration, the addict usually seeks out crisis
relating and crisis situations. When the addict becomes desensitized
even to these crises, he or she *creates* crisis, without conscious
awareness of motivation or responsibility for the situation. Crisis
relating involves seeking a partner with whom crises are inevitable.
Severe stimulation addicts may choose to be with severely disturbed
people: drug addicts, alcoholics, severely dependent people,
chronic gamblers, etc. Or they may choose people with whom they
can readily get into crisis situations of their own making—border-
line illegalities, for instance, or stressful business ventures.

One of the most common responses to stimulation addiction
is seeking new and unfamiliar relationships. Indeed, being "locked
into" one relationship, for whatever reason, may cause severe anxiety and depression for the stimulation addict. The need for new
relationships often precludes the possibility of long-term relating
on a fruitful level. When forced into long-term relating, the addict
feels severely coerced and often responds with conscious rage motivated by underlying addictive needs of which he knows nothing
at all. He may try to start arguments to add drama to the relationship; he may turn to vindictive and sadistic displays against his
partner—anything to provide stimulation. Needless to say, this
behavior undermines any kind of cooperative relationship.

The stimulation addict tends to view lesser addicts, let alone nonaddicts, as resigned, cowardly, boring "dead heads." He also tends to spread his addiction to those around him—especially his children. He will teach them to feel sorry for the "dead heads" and admire the so-called live ones—a lesson mainly successful with children and morbidly dependent or compulsively compliant adults. Healthy people usually have no interest in what they perceive as shallow, superficial living, and so stimulation addicts rarely find relatively healthy people with whom to sustain relationships.

Obviously, the tendency toward destruction is very strong in people who have been unduly influenced by stimulation addiction. They tend to destroy relationships—their own and others; they also tend to form relationships that are inherently destructive from the outset. Too often they live mainly in their imaginations, where exaggerated versions of real life provide some relief when actual stimulation is missing. But this is followed by repeated disappointment with real life, real people, and real relating partners. Too often, they exhaust themselves and their partners in attempts to sustain excitement at any cost. They contrive all kinds of situations that may be stimulating: for example, I have known a number of people who secretly encouraged infidelities on the part of mates in order to risk loss as well as to contrive grievances and crisis.

Living between stations, so to speak, as the stimulation addict does, means arranging life so as to be in a constant state of upheaval—geographically, professionally, economically, socially, and emotionally. This is utterly destructive to relating on a deep, sustained level. If your calendar, or your partner's, is booked down to the last minute six weeks ahead, stimulation addiction is your problem. It is time to think about taking a different kind of risk—a risk of being alone with yourself.

Misha and Mindy

It was love at first sight for each of them, and they've been married for almost thirty years. They consider themselves "a fun couple," but all of a sudden it isn't so much fun. Something has nagged at their relationship from the beginning and now threatens to upset them for real.

The problem is that they have never been able to stand the idea of not being able to afford what they've wanted—and they've always wanted a great deal. They both love cars, restaurants, clothes, theater, traveling, and lots of everything else. And they've always found it hard to say *no* to themselves. They just have to have what they want, and throughout their married lives they've been hounded by bill collectors.

Misha is a would-be wheeler-dealer, and Mindy has helped him in the many businesses they've tried. But these have never panned out, and the result has been numerous lawsuits, bankruptcies, and a "lot of other stuff that isn't fun at all." Their credit with banks and stores is currently zero. They've "not gambled or anything like that," even though they both admit that most of their ventures were pretty big gambles and "showed poor judgment."

Throughout everything, though, they got along well together. There was a short period a few years back when they were very upset with each other and drifted apart for a while. They describe having at that time gone through a kind of "mid-life crisis"—each went off and had an affair, which didn't last, and they were happy to get back together again.

Now they are growing frightened. They want to settle down to something solid. They are in their mid-fifties and can't see how they can possibly live on social security. Misha wonders how things would have turned out if they had "really made it." He still envies people who did. He thinks their lives are more interesting, and imagines that they don't age as he and Mindy are doing.

This is a fairly cooperative relationship—one based on shared assumptions about what to strive for in life. Together they bought the stimulation addict's bill of goods, and now they're frightened of the "dead" future that confronts them. Because they're cooperative, and mutually supportive, they have a better chance than most relating couples to kick the stimulation habit—even though it was that cooperativeness that led them into their predicament in the first place.

YOUTH ORIENTATION, SUPERFICIALITY, AND AFFECTATION

Liking somebody's voice, or the way they dance or drive a car or order food in a restaurant, or the way they dress and the impression they seem to make on others, or the way they hold a cigarette, is not basis for a real relationship: these things must not be confused with values, tastes, real interests, personal development; with the ability to be open, tender, intimate, trusting, and caring; with proclivity for being deeply involved, invested, and committed.

Yet our deodorized culture would have us believe that superficial attributes are the very stuff of relating life, that relating partners are show-and-tell objects whose principal function is to glitter brightly enough that other people will admire them. Any woman who has been used in this way will tell you how much like a whole human being she feels. Yet many attempts at long-standing, involved relationships—including many marriages—are based on superficialities and cultural symbols of attraction. In these relationships expectation of immediate gratification and poor frustration tolerance combine to make the relationship itself even more fragmenting and unlikely to survive very long. Enormous concentration of time and energy is spent in affectation and posing. Indeed, there are relationships in which relating consists almost totally of striking poses and developing new affectations. This is done by each partner to the other, and by both in concert to impress others. Some people play out entire roles and develop new ones as they go along. Think of the couple in which one partner plays the little girl and the other the daddy; then she becomes the joiner of causes, the earthshaker, and expects him (although he doesn't know the script) to follow suit and become her disciple or her comrade-in-arms. Some even dress alike, in an effort to find a costume for the role that life represents to them. (This kind of behavior can also go on between parent and child. One of my patients felt terribly exploited by her mother, who had spent hours costuming her so that she would supplement the mother's concept of herself as a "grande dame." She remembered, with enormous sustained resentment, sitting for hours as a restless three-year-old while her hair was perfectly arranged and she was dressed in stiff little dresses that complemented her mother's outfits.) These people often hang out together, vying with each other for the position of best-dressed, wealthiest, best party-giver. Their relationships—their performing partnerships—are sustained as long as they are able to influence each other and outsiders. But they hardly know each other and are in terror of knowing themselves. They become increasingly bored and cynical. Is it any wonder that they often turn to destructive acts, including suicide?

One of their major affectations is a preoccupation with looking and staying young. A youth obsession is utterly self-defeating and obviously oriented against reality—we *must* get older if we live. Youth orientation denies this, and thereby fosters self-hate and hatred for the people with whom we relate. It feeds our desire for stimulation addiction. It adds to contempt for older people and deprives them of dignity and the possibility of fruitful and healthy relationships. It denigrates the value of experience. It works against life itself, promoting the myth of the short happy life. It promotes a kind of narcissistic self-preoccupation that cuts us off from the possibility of real exchange with ourselves and others. It makes our own mortality and all the limitations of humanity abhorrent.

Expending time and energy for posing, affectation, and superficial living leaves little or no possibility of making *real* emotional investments in our partners. Without such a real emotional investment, relationships are shallow and unsatisfying. Ultimately they become boring, and the relating partners make frenetic attempts to dilute their boredom by collecting more and more people, experiences, and things. But these do not alleviate that sense of emptiness, because they aren't experienced fully and deeply. And so the vicious circle of affectation and superficial relationships continues.

ME FIRST

The label of the "Me decade," pinned on the 1970s, might also be applied to our present-day society. Social autism or self-preoccupation has come to be viewed as a kind of self-caring or self-enrichment; but it is really a form of narcissistic detachment, an alienation from others, and the antithesis of real self-interest. Ultimately it spells disaster for relationships.

Always saying "me first," as our competitive society encourages us to do, makes us ignore the feelings, values, personal priorities, tastes, and choices of others with whom we might have deeper relationships. Compassion for self involves self-acceptance; it means acceptance of *all* aspects of the human condition—including those feelings and qualities of which we are ashamed; it does not hinge on achievement. The "me first" psychology is totally achievement-oriented.

Compassionate relating with others is a natural consequence of compassionate relating with oneself. Compassionate relating invariably involves the smaller, mundane details of life in which decisions are shared with a cooperative partner. This is the antithesis of "me first." But as long as people equate self-preoccupation with real self-love, real compassion for self, the possibilities for fruitful relating are slim indeed.

POPULARITY AND CELEBRITY: THE COMPULSIVE NEED TO BE LIKED

In our society, popularity and fame are thought to guarantee against loneliness and boredom. Being popular is equated with success. Parents, from the earliest times in their children's lives, are terribly concerned with popularity. Winning the prize for being the most popular boy or girl in school often outshines any other achievement. And celebrity is confused with expertise; it is not unusual to see movie stars and other celebrities on television shows making pronouncements on matters political, sociological, or psychological about which they know little or nothing.

To be the most popular we must play to the crowd—we become actors, and the act becomes more important than the real thing. We lose touch with who we are; we need the crowd for a sense of identification and orientation. Without popularity and celebrity some of us have hardly any selves at all. Think what this does to our relationships! It promotes the kind of relating exemplified by a person who looks over your shoulder as he talks to you, always concerned about meeting other people or about his effect on other people. In this kind of relationship no real exchanges can take place.

We are taught that to be liked, to be nice, is of critical importance. It *is* critically important—in its destructive impact on our lives. Being nice too often means being a mirror image for other people: they get nothing from us except what *they* put in. And it sets up a painful contradiction, because being liked and being self-assertive are both given great value in our society. It is not possible to be universally liked and self-assertive at the same time, since we confuse self-assertion with aggression, and aggression always involves putting the next guy down. As one woman I saw recently asked, "After all, who doesn't want to be liked—or better yet loved—by everyone? Who doesn't want to be popular and famous, too?" She had come to see me because she wanted to learn how to assert herself. She said that she had terrible anxiety when she even tried and would feel depressed afterward, regardless of whether she did or didn't. Her conflict was obvious to me but not to her.

There is a further danger to relationships in the compulsive need to be liked. Karen Horney, the great anatomist of character structure, described the inevitable links between it and the condition she called morbid dependency or morbid self-effacement. Morbid self-effacement occurs when our security and self-esteem have been so shaken that we feel we must always tiptoe through life, being nice, conforming, and "good," not making waves, in order to be loved. Indeed, love is seen as the solution to all problems. Some self-effacement can produce duplicity, frustration, and disturbance in relationships, because we simply cannot serve two or more masters: we cannot often please ourselves and others at the same time. And we pay a heavy price when we negate ourselves in the service of being liked: sacrifice of self leaves little self with which to relate. Repression of our own identities eventually results in being out of touch with real feelings and desires. As dependency increases directly proportional to loss of self, impossible claims, usually in the name of love, are made on the partner. And when these claims are thwarted, rage and more repression are the result.

People who are seriously self-effacing and compulsively compliant attempt to "read other people" and then to feed back what they believe their relating partners want to hear. It is anathema to them to tell it like it is, to communicate what they really feel and believe, let alone what they desire. Often, they simply don't know. They are out of practice. Their messages constantly change with the person to whom the message is delivered. Dealing with a "nonentity," a constantly changing mirror image, is never satisfying for the self-effacing person's partner, and it is frustrating. But self-effacing people cannot understand the other person's dissatisfaction; they feel they have sacrificed themselves totally for love, never realizing that it isn't love at all, only a compulsive need to be liked in order to feel safe.

JUSTICE, GUILT, REWARD, PUNISHMENT, RESPONSIBILITY

In a healthy, cooperative relationship we do not sit in judgment on our partner for having human characteristics, limitations, or confusions that our culture deems less than ideal. We struggle to accept all that is human in ourselves and our relating partners without moralizing or punishing them for their seeming or actual shortcomings. But unfortunately our society is motivated by a quest for justice and obsessed with the laws of evidence, guilt, innocence, reward, and punishment. And we treat ourselves and each other accordingly.

In a relationship, ascribing fault, making reparations, and generating guilt all produce continuing, chronic hostility. If a wife fails to have a satisfying sexual response and blames her husband, this doesn't help alleviate the situation; the focus becomes fixed on a battle to establish who is right and who is wrong in the relationship, rather than on the relating problems themselves.

Occasionally, I see couples who have been chronically assaulting each other. Most often, each claims that the other is at fault, and they attempt to make me the judge, to ascribe guilt, and to contribute to vindication through further vilification. I usually point out that since neither one is responsible, responsibility has obviously fallen somewhere on the floor between them. Until each person picks up his or her share, no progress can be made toward remediation. This is what I call "the floor phenomenon."

One of the principal characteristics of a healthy family is the emphasis on needs and assets. This means that individuals must relate unburdened by claims for justice, rights, equal sharing, and the paranoid preoccupation of making sure "I get mine." In this kind of family, individual needs are respected, and individual assets or abilities and talents are used effectively. Unfortunately, sibling rivalry often arises when competitive parents encourage a narcissistic preoccupation with justice on the part of their children. Each child worries obsessively that he or she may get a smaller piece of the pie than his brothers and sisters. This means that when *real* needs are at issue, and one family member needs more than the others, great hostility is engendered in a family governed by the need for ruthless equality. This striving for equality also causes families to overlook the natural abilities of its members, and to try to tap resources that are not there: if one child shows musical talent but there isn't enough money for piano lessons for *both* children, the parents decide that *neither* will take piano lessons because equal treatment is more important than individual needs.

Sibling rivalry, preoccupation with ruthless equality, and justice based on guilt or innocence and leading to reward and punishment tend to fragment a family as its members encapsulate themselves and become ruthless isolationists. This is, to say the least, a poor practice for future relating. Small wonder that in so many adult marriages money is not shared but is individually owned. As we shall see, money is a potent symbol: we often find that in those marriages and families little else is shared either, particularly trust. The preoccupation with the abstractions of justice and responsibility has taken over, often causing neglect of individual needs and the real human substance that nourishes a healthy relationship.

NEUROTIC PRIDE

No facet of human behavior can be more devastating to relating than those that function in the service of pride. Pride deserves a whole book—indeed, Karen Horney spent a lifetime brilliantly describing this human phenomenon in all her works—but we must attempt here to discuss it briefly, in the context of human relationships.

For my purpose there is no such thing as healthy pride. That which is called healthy pride is actually a form of self-realization, or the satisfaction that comes from self-realization. This satisfaction has nothing to do with feeling vulnerable; with anxiety; with obsessive, compulsive quests for unrealistic, impossible goals; with achieving superiority over others, with forcing others to comply with our own inner contractual agreements. Self-realization does not make demands on relating partners. But pride does all these things.

Our society constantly bombards us with pride messages—pride in country, pride in self, pride in looks, achievement, winning, greatness. Culture dictates areas for "pride investment."

These include pride invested in strength, in being smart, in power, in being popular, in being young, in looks, in mastery, in martyrdom, in sexuality, in racial and national identity. In all these areas, pride is the great cover-up, the great shield. It hides from us our real selves, both our human limitations and our assets. It distorts our view of ourselves. It wrecks inner peace and is highly destructive to real relating. The Greeks knew this well—what else are their great tragedies about but the sin of pride?

Pride is directly proportional to low self-esteem, insecurity, anxiety, and fear. It is the antithesis of real inner strength, humility, and self-realization. It is the generator of self-hate, rage, depression, suicide, murder, paranoia, and war—the greatest social malignancy of all.

The human condition dictates insecurity. Anxiety is also a concomitant of being human and alive. But if we are taught to shun both, we become anxious about being insecure and about being anxious. This snowball effect makes anxiety intolerable. We are taught to deal with this intolerable state—of real humanity—by covering up with a mantle of pride. We construct a false, idealized, proud image of ourselves in order to hide our real selves, real feelings, real limits, and real humanity from ourselves.

In so doing, we learn to hate ourselves, and this self-hate is indeed the dynamo that keeps pride and the quest for glory going. Reminders of how we fall short of our idealized self in any area of pride investment—looks, wealth, achievement, whatever—will bring on attacks of self-hate. For example, a businessman who has pride invested in always making excellent decisions, and who in fact is terrified of really being stupid and helpless, will experience a business failure as a great blow to his pride. This will put him in touch with real self-limitations and with self-hate. If his self-hate is severe enough, serious emotional depression will ensue.

But quite often intolerable self-hate is projected or displaced to other people, especially to the seeming perpetrators of the hurt pride, and the result is that the individual whose pride is hurt will feel rage against the other. Our businessman, to continue the example, will feel anger at his associates for giving him faulty information, or at his opponents for conspiring to ruin him.

How is pride destructive to relationships? In several ways.

Pride is known in parts of the world as "saving face." In this frame of reference, face or surface—how we seem to others—is more important than what we really are. Trying to relate to this surface person without hurting the sensitive areas of his pride can be extremely wearisome, self-depleting, self-denigrating, and duplicitous. Obviously, when prideful people relate, they often get into "pride deadlocks," a situation in which neither gives way and the relationship dissolves with many hurt feelings. But pride often works in subtle ways on a relatively unconscious level where situations that may make hurt pride possible are carefully avoided. I know one man who refused to go to certain parties to which he was invited with seemingly no rhyme or reason while he attended others readily. "Just my feeling, that's all," he said. On investigation it turned out that he avoided all parties in which people who made more money than he would be present. As he became aware of his problem and worked to overcome it, his pride in making money was relinquished; his self-acceptance was no longer predicated on money earned. (And he began going out without fear of meeting someone who made more than he did.)

There are two responses to hurt pride that are highly destructive to relating—on an individual and on a global level. One is to attempt to restore pride through vengeance or "getting even," through scoring a vindictive triumph and "showing them." Fantasies of "showing them," "making them eat dirt," can often be traced to early youth and even childhood—but they are learned in a society that is constantly preoccupied with balancing scales. Extreme examples would be Hitler, Stalin, or Napoleon; more mundanely, we see this kind of behavior in the unpopular man who, when he gets control of his company, fires everybody subordinate to him. What kind of relationship can he have with his professional associates?

Withdrawal is even more malignant to relationships. We discussed this mechanism in the section about anger—and indeed, withdrawal *is* one way of showing anger in a relationship. But mainly withdrawal restores *pride* as it attempts to restore an attitude of superiority: "I can get along perfectly well without any of you." This mechanism is often found in sulking children, who symbolically and in actuality often have a history of responding to hurt pride by "taking their marbles and going home," depriving others of their presence. The ultimate withdrawal is suicide, in which the other person is made to feel sorry, and guilty too, and the suicide shows his prideful contempt for partaking in the lowly life of the living.

Pride causes relating partners to make all kinds of inappropriate claims on other people in the service of what is felt as being due them. The message is, "You owe me all kinds of demonstrations that show you recognize my special status." For example, a man who has pride invested in being a great lover makes claims on women to succumb to his charms and to respond rapturously to his lovemaking. When they don't, he feels his position as a great lover is threatened: he is put in touch with his self-hate, which he then projects onto the woman in question. He rages at her and attempts to restore his pride position as a great lover by blaming her vindictively for her lack of response. Such claims are often consciously felt as ethically, morally, legally, and in every way justifiable.

Where pride has not polluted a relationship, extraordinary measures to communicate need not be taken. Messages are straight and clear-cut; they are designed neither to avoid hurting pride nor to manipulate to serve pride. Misunderstandings are easily remedied. People know what they feel and what they want, and their messages are used to convey real information about what they really feel and want.

When pride is seriously damaged and depression ensues, one of two courses is taken. Pride may be gradually repaired and reestablished—through vindictive fantasies of "showing them" or by withdrawing, picking up the marbles and going home—or it may be recognized and relinquished. When people change and grow in the direction of health, the battle to relinquish pride is launched. As this takes place, as pride is surrendered, our real selves emerge.

The Bassets—"The Proud Outsiders"

They haven't "made it," although her sister and his brother and sister are all successful, live in large houses, have big cars and lots of money. One is even a well-known writer. But the Bassets are not successful themselves. They know they are smart. Their parents and their teachers always told them so. But somehow they couldn't use their intelligence to achieve what they consider success.

They live well enough, but in comparison to the others they feel they have very little. They demean everything they have, and they put down everything everyone else has, too. Their three teen-age children have as little to do with them as possible, but—being the victims of victims as so many of us tend to be—they already demonstrate some of their parents' attitudes and behavior.

The Bassets are semireclusive: they socialize minimally and are chronically angry at their relatives and the rest of the world. They can't get along with their parents or their other relatives and don't keep friends for very long. They believe that the world, their family, other people owe them more than what they get. They feel abused and sooner or later victimized by anyone they come into contact with. Out of this delusion they have developed a sense of superiority through martyrdom—them against the world. Their shared feeling of being specially picked out for bad luck binds them to each other with strong mutual dependency. The rest of the world, it seems, fails to recognize their uniqueness and does not make special allowances for them; and this attitude often spills over to their children. Theirs is an unhappy, relatively seclusive, morose household. Actually their lives are dedicated to sustaining a perverse pride position. In essence, they have picked up their marbles and gone home. Even as they continue to envy other people, they are harboring the illusion that they are superior, "above it all." They have a pseudo-cooperative relationship with each other based on an antagonistic relationship with the world and the human condition generally.

Their isolation and bitterness have alienated them from their family and friends, and made them ignore their own inner resources. They are so busy feeling superior about nothing that they have no time or energy to devote to becoming *something*, and the cycle of their isolation and unhappiness is perpetuated.

COMPETITION AND
SUCCESS

There is virtually no dynamic force in society as destructive to relationships—through erosion of the individual and through attack on the relating unit—as competitive striving.

As I've stated elsewhere, I do not believe that our species is instinctively competitive, aggressive, or inclined toward a territorial imperative of any kind. I do not believe that sibling rivalry is instinctive or genetic. Like all other aspects of competitive living, it is *learned*. We compete, we fight wars, we are compulsively concerned about our hierarchical position relative to the next person, because we learn to be so through a psychotic culture passed on from one generation to the next.

Competition simply does not bring out the best in us; it brings out the worst. When we are more interested in the ends than the means, the product than the process, we denigrate involvement of real self in doing good, self-realizing work. A competitive, hierarchical society imposes performance standards, conditions, and criteria for self-acceptance. Failure to keep up with the proverbial Joneses in any area leads to self-rejection and all of its consequences to self and to relationships.

Once criteria for self-acceptance are established, failure to accept ourselves is guaranteed. This is so because, as with all self-glorifying devices, the standards get higher and higher until failure inevitably ensues. It is simply impossible to beat all of our competitors all of the time. Punishment for failure takes the form of self-hate, depression, self-recrimination, weakening of self, heightened vulnerability and fragility, and all the subsequent damage to relationships that ensues.

The competitive drive is a cruel and obsessive taskmaster that demands our total attention: for the competitive workaholic, time spent away from competitive goals, with family or friends, for example, is time spent with feelings of anxiety and guilt. Competition also makes us narrow specialists because it takes specialization to compete. This further deprives us of other interests that might help us—the compulsively competitive engineer never takes time for museums, reading, music. What kind of relationships can such people enjoy?

When we compete, the center of gravity of our emotional lives shifts radically from within us to outside ourselves. In effect, we turn over our entire identifying, motivating force to the person or persons or institutions in competition with us. We are really saying that inasmuch as we must get ahead of "him," *he* determines where and what we have to achieve.

This compulsive reaction to an outside influence destroys our own spontaneity, our ability to be in touch with inside music, as it were. This process insidiously destroys inner feelings, linkages to inner resources, personal values, and one's own frame of reference. It has a severely deleterious effect on one's identifying structure, as it weakens and empties the self. Couples caught in tandem in the competitive process often have empty relationships and function in robotlike fashion in pursuit of competitors who dictate the terms of their lives and their activities.

As an externalizing force, competition prevents us from really getting to know the other person, who becomes a screen on whom we project and loses validity to us as the real person he or she is. Projection or externalization makes for more than distortion. The attributes we project onto our partners obliterate the reality of who they really are; we are, in fact, relating to our own projected goals and taskmasters, as well as to the standards the other person seemingly has achieved, rather than to real people.

Finally, the competitive drive locks us into something I call the cooperation/competition conflict, a trap I discovered some time ago in treating patients. I believe that as relating creatures people have a natural proclivity and need to cooperate. This need is inherent in the fact that the newborn cannot take care of himself for many years. This need is the basis for familial relating, and extends into the community at large, forming a cornerstone of what we come to know as society and culture.

But the pressure to compete even as we desire to cooperate splits us in two, creating great internal conflict and severe anxiety. We simply can't cooperate and compete at the same time. Attempting cooperation with a colleague and at the same time looking over our shoulder constantly to make sure he doesn't get ahead of us contributes to paranoia. The attempt to compete outside and then to cooperate at home usually fails and makes for unsatisfactory relating in both places. I do not believe that sibling rivalry is genetic or instinctual. I believe it is learned from competing parents who unconsciously pass on messages to their children instructing them to compete. Parents also unwittingly compete with each other and with their children, extending competition into family life and precluding real cooperation. The splits or conflicts make for chronic disquietude and a sense of guilt, because one part of us is unhappy as the other part is served. The attempt to remedy this untenable situation is, as I explained earlier in the chapter on sadomasochism, to engage antagonistically in sadomasochistic relationships as a comprehensive solution in which both taskmasters are served, one at a time, pseudo-satisfactorily.

V

THE CURRENCY
OF RELATING

HOW RELATIONSHIPS
REVEAL THEMSELVES

There are myriad manifestations that arise from the rich substance of our basic relating potential. There are also complications that are bound to come up as extensions of individual needs combined with cultural pressures. I call these secondary elaborations the *currency* of relating, the everyday coinage with which we deal with one another: money, sex, time, leadership, and a host of other things. Of course, confusions are bound to arise about the values represented by this currency: money is sometimes more than money, sex is almost always more than sex, and feelings can be expressed—and interpreted—in a variety of ways.

In these next pages I shall describe some of the most common elaborations—the possibilities are almost infinite. I shall also try to clarify some of the complications and confusions, and in some cases to further extend our understanding of the basic psychodynamics already discussed. Up to now we have described relationships in terms of the relating partners, character structures, and influences that make the relationships what they are. Now we will talk about how they *work* in our everyday lives.

MONEY

The way couples manage their money often tells more about certain deep, unconscious aspects of a relationship in our money-conscious society than anything else. Where money is seen as symbolic blood, intelligence, power, or self-esteem, to say that it is a commodity in which there is an emotional investment is putting it mildly.

Feelings about money are extremely powerful. More often than not, even the deepest, longest, closest friendships succumb to the special feelings involving money. This is clearly demonstrated by the fact that many friends refuse to lend money, and even fewer will give it to each other (except in ritualized ways—weddings, etc.), however much they have and however great the need. Indeed, they will sooner give blood! In our society one's money is sacred. The further fact is that very few friends, however close, will be open about the amount of money they have. Almost everything else may be shared, but money matters constitute secret information.

The reason that money is so expressive a commodity in any

relationship is the pride inherent in financial status—as well as the potential for hurt pride. Battles over money in a relationship are usually battles over position, pride, and general control. Financial crises, sudden money depletions and pressures, provide stress situations that reveal much. Does the couple respond as a cooperative, mutually supportive team? Or do they respond vindictively, with recriminations, externalizations, and claims?

In relationships with children, as well as with mates, money is easily used to manipulate, to punish, to reward, to frustrate, to tempt, to blackmail.

So what goes on with money tells us more than what goes on with money: the couple who guard their separate monies and continue to sustain separate net worths, separate fiscal controls, and separate bank accounts have more often than not withheld capitulation and commitment to the relationship. Their mutual trust may indeed be in question. Their capacity for openness and emotional sharing may have large limitations.

Wives who receive "allowances," who are kept in the dark about money matters, who are not full partners in money decisions, are often infantilized generally and are sustained in a dependent position. Statements like "I'll have to ask John if I can have it" or "It's his money—after all, he earns it, so it's only right that he is the boss of it" are usually a giveaway. This childlike status extends into all matters of treatment, and all family decision making, though this may not be at once apparent.

Mates who refuse to understand, let alone participate in money matters, may be acting out the role of the child in all aspects of the relationship, or may be expressing considerable general emotional detachment. Some narcissistic, infantile people want to be brought gifts, but want nothing that resembles monetary involvement. Some highly sexist women see money matters as strictly the responsibility of the male and want no part of fiscal problems. We often find that these people compartmentalize their lives generally along sex gender lines.

Cooperative, democratic, mature, responsibility-sharing, emotionally involved and committed people almost always demonstrate their cooperation through their equal participation and sharing of power in money matters. So if you are looking for a fast readout of how a particular relationship works, ask what role money plays in it.

Brown vs. Brown

It was all about money. When they married she had too much of it; he did not earn enough of it. Her father was a rich man and insisted on her starting married life with a large sum of money of her own. And he meant "her own." After all, he said, "you never know how a marriage turns out—he looks like a great guy, but the money must remain in your name." And that's how it was for twenty-seven years.

Aside from their money differences, their cultural backgrounds were essentially similar. They were both third-generation Americans. They both had college educations. They both came from stable family backgrounds. They had similar tastes and were both family- and children-oriented. The big difference was the money. Not that the husband came from an impoverished background. His family had always lived well. Both he and his brother were put through law school without having to work, and they really wanted for nothing. But they simply never became rich.

Tim Brown went on to make a very good living, eventually becoming a partner in a "fairly good" law firm. But he felt like a "poor relative" from the beginning and continued to sustain this feeling about himself throughout their marriage. Their financial arrangement was fairly simple and straightforward. They lived off his income. His wife Janet's money remained "her money," and she "gave him extra money when he needed it for extra things," like the children's schooling and camp, the extra medical bills that came up, the new car, or her fur coats (she paid for them, but he bought them as a "present" for her). Her money made money, and so she became richer as time went on. His finances remained unchanged, since he could never accumulate enough to invest.

After the first few months their relationship became antagonistic and acrimonious. He said that money was more important to her than he was. She said that the money was used as they needed it and that it wasn't as if she used it only for herself. He felt that they should manage it together and even own it jointly.

She said that this would be contrary to her father's wishes; furthermore, under direction from her father, she had invested very wisely—wasn't this for their common good? She said he wasn't aggressive enough in his professional life. He accused her of insensitivity and of being excessively materialistic. She said he was essentially lazy and, unlike the men in *her* family, didn't really know what being the man in the family was all about.

These "money fights" gradually metastasized to all areas of their lives, so that they agreed about nothing and rejected each other's tastes, opinions, desires, ideas in all matters large and small. They couldn't agree on what movies to see, on how to bring up the children, on what friends to be with, on what vacations to take. Over the years "money fights" seemed to become just one of a great list of mutual complaints and recriminations.

She secretly hated him for not earning enough to nullify the power of her father's money, thus allowing her to transfer her feelings for her father to him. He felt that she had never really accepted their relationship and that she had never had confidence in him. He externalized and blamed her for his inability to "make it big" in his professional world because she had undermined his self-confidence.

When they divorced, their mutual hatred grew to almost psychotic proportions. And it was all there to be seen from the beginning, in the way they managed their money.

Harry, Dorothy, and Sam

Harry and Dorothy are married and have three small children; they are both seeing psychoanalytic therapists. Harry has always made "good money," and during ten years of marriage their income has increased regularly. They "are very happy together," "have won-derful kids," and talk out and resolve problems constructively. They are open, tender, trusting, and intimate with each other and their children; the children are happy, love school, and get along with their friends. But it wasn't always this way—there was a time, prior to their marriage, when both Harry and Dorothy had difficulties with feelings of inadequacy and getting along with people. Dorothy in particular was severely depressed, insecure, and self-hating. Treatment helped them a great deal, and they now lead active, happy social lives, too.

Their big problem area is money. It has always been that way. No matter how much money Harry earns, it is never enough. The kids need private school. Then there's their treatment—and taxes and inflation. The car is a big expense in New York, "parking and repairs cost a lot," but they "use it often to entertain the kids" in nearby country spots they couldn't get to otherwise. Besides, they're used to it—they've always had a car. Then there are doctor bills and other things. "Something always comes up, and always costs money."

Dorothy's father, Sam, who's a successful businessman, gives them money. He also gives them a "hard time," but they always get the money, too—"not enough to invest or anything like that, no steady amount either," but enough for each crisis that comes up. And they "always do come up." Sam's "hard time" consists of a lecture in which he vilifies psychotherapy, suggesting that they drop it, and tells them that they are living beyond their means and must cut down. Although Sam makes his living investing and han-dling other people's money, he never discusses money management on a practical basis with them. He just lectures them and then produces the handout.

Dorothy is one of three children, but has always felt that she was her father's favorite. Indeed, many of the difficulties that brought her to treatment were due to early, severe overprotection, which she interpreted as love. This kind of overprotection has little to do with love and is largely a function of parental insecurity and anxiety displaced to the child, who is felt as a vulnerable part of an extended self. Overprotection is stifling, and in Dorothy's case it sustained a feeling of vulnerability and fragility into adulthood.

Harry, on the other hand, came from a family that he felt was overpermissive: parents who just "didn't care all that much." He felt this was particularly true of his father, a rather detached, seclusive person. Since he could remember, Harry had envied boys who had close, strong relationships with their fathers.

So when Sam lectured Harry and Dorothy, and when, later, he gave them the money, Harry wasn't unhappy to play son to Sam's "Dad." In fact, both Harry and Dorothy enjoyed playing siblings, playing house, under the protective aegis of Sam, the benevolent father to both "children." For his part, Sam's unconscious goal was to infantilize Dorothy, and he was willing enough to adopt Harry too, as part of this pact. Sam has succeeded—with the willing cooperation of Dorothy and Harry. Harry always wanted a different kind of father than he had, and he got one. Dorothy did not want to let go of the one she had, and she didn't. Harry and Dorothy continued to sustain their essential dependency, while Sam used them to sustain his mastery.

But Harry and Dorothy's psychiatric therapy represented, especially to Sam, a potential threat to this status quo. In a way the psychiatrists became a rival set of parents—"bad parents"—for Harry and Dorothy. Sam would jealously vilify and try to undermine them; the young people, Harry and Dorothy, would report these rantings to the doctors, using the reports as vehicles for venting their own anger at their therapists. After all, they too were secretly angry at therapy, since it threatened to end their dependency.

In this case money was the big manipulative tool, and all three used it accordingly. Sam's use of it was obvious. He never helped them to really extricate themselves or to manage properly, and always "came through." Dorothy and Harry did their bit by faithfully spending just a bit more than they could afford, no matter how much they had. And one of the main areas of money difficulty was their therapy fees. This was the subject about which Sam lectured most, and these fees generally were given low payment priority by Dorothy and Harry, so that there was always a considerable accumulated bill with which to stimulate Sam periodically. All three of them used money as the language with which to express their feelings about themselves and one another.

SEX

The sex lives of couples may or may not be extensions of their relating lives generally. The chemistry of sexual attraction in our society often has more to do with symbols and conditioning than it has to do with relatedness and love. We are taught to respond to certain sexual stimuli, often on a subliminal level (large breasts, black hair, a certain swagger), and go on responding even when no real exchange of feelings is taking place. This is especially true for people who are more alienated, less in touch with their feelings, than others, and are therefore unable to integrate sexual feelings and relatedness.

There are people whose only constructive relating takes place in their sex lives together. Some are thoroughly antagonistic and almost ritualistically sadomasochistic in all other areas of their lives, but gentle, loving, and responsive to each other's stimuli and sexual needs. Indeed, some function sexually only after their most scathing attacks on each other take place: it is as if they needed these excoriations to break down pride and let sexually stimulating feelings come through. For some of these people, their everyday antagonistic behavior acts as foreplay and is a function of sexual need. But there are also others who are warm and tender out of bed and unrelentingly brutal and sadistic in bed, needing the in-fliction of physical pain and degradation to activate deadened sex-ual feelings.

Freud believed that neurotic difficulties are the result of sexual problems arising from early unresolved sexual feelings for one's par-ents and ensuing repression of sexual urges. If this were true, the examination of behavioral difficulties would eventually lead us to a sexual cause. While this may be true in some cases, I hold with just the reverse point of view. I believe that sexual life is largely an extension of how we relate generally and that sexual problems are often reflections of relating difficulties. Of course, this is not always the case. Sometimes physiological problems do exist. Sometimes confusion and ignorance produce problems, too. But for the most part, sexual behavior is consistent with other behavior, and ex-amination of how people behave sexually may often tell us some-thing of what *really* transpires between them generally.

Sexual behavior can indicate what underlying feelings tran-spire between participants much more accurately than their general behavior does. I have known a number of severely self-effacing, dependent, compliant women who frustrate and even denigrate their partners in bed, the one place in which repressed hostility can take active form. Some of the most self-effacing people use sex as reward and punishment, and as a means of restoring hurt pride. I have also known a number of compliant men who are sadistically aggressive in their "lovemaking."

Some people who are ordinarily repressed and reserved dem-onstrate enormous warmth and tenderness through sex. Often the seemingly passive partner in a relationship is nearly always the sex-ual initiator and is indeed the quiet power behind the throne in all matters. This, of course, does not usually appear to be so to friends, or even to the couple themselves. Many people act out ceremonial closeness with many "dears" and "darlings" for friends, but are ac-tually distant in terms of their feelings for each other, and this is amply demonstrated by complete sexual coldness.

Understanding what goes on sexually in a relationship can often help us to get beneath the surface of superficial behavior. For example, Freudians believe that women who dream they have a penis suffer from "penis envy" and actually desire to own that anatomical organ. We of other schools of thought believe that the penis is a symbol of power in a power-ridden culture. We believe that many women who dream of having a penis desire more power generally in the everyday business of their lives. Unlike orthodox Freudians, we believe that castration anxiety has little to do with fear of loss of the organ and much to do with fear of loss of power in general.

Singling out sex as the only or as the prime vehicle for relating information may lead to considerable confusion rather than to clarification. This is not unlike the interpretation of dreams in which the dream opens up and tells much, but only if we understand the meaning of the symbols in terms of the individual dreamer and his or her life.

Many overtly sexual dreams, in fact, give more information about general relating feelings and activity than they do about the actual sex life of the dreamer. Dreamers may use sex to cover up other feelings, and also as a means of expressing strong emotions, since their sexual feelings are their strongest ones. I am reminded of a self-effacing man who repressed great anger toward his aggressive wife. In actuality, he was very passive sexually. In his dreams his sexual activity took the form of extremely strong movements. His associations to the dream revealed that intercourse represented his "letting her have it" and really telling her off. The sweetness he demonstrated vis-à-vis her turned out to be a charade, a cover-up of his hostile feelings, which were revealed by his sexual dreams. This man's considerable anxiety was relieved as he began to accept and to deal with his anger on a healthier basis. As this happened, his relationship with his wife became more honest, more interesting, and more constructive.

Diana's Dilemma

She can't seem to "make it with any man."

She is extremely attractive, beautiful actually, vivacious, talented, and bright. She attracts many men. Those who are not overwhelmed by her obvious charms almost invariably want to go out with her, to be with her. She is a responsive, vibrant person.

More than anything she wants "a sustained relationship." But one just never works out. "Either it just doesn't take off at all or in no time at all we're fighting and it's a downhill course—down and out. So many of them are just not there; they're with you, but they're not with you. Others are so weak. They can't make up their minds about anything. They can't make any decisions. They don't know where to go, what to do—you know, the so-called boring nice guys. What turnoffs! The interesting ones—feisty, talented, alive—can't live and let live. They get into your life; they want to take over entirely. Then you've got to cater to them. Underneath it all, they've got this damned macho shtick. Have to be told how good, how wonderful they are a million times a day. God, isn't there some interesting, grownup, normal, regular guy around? Or is it all me?"

Diana externalizes her own unreconciled intrapsychic conflict to the men she forms relationships with. She is overtly expansive and narcissistic, but although she has repressed her own self-effacement and detachment, these trends are powerful in her—and they are brought out by the men she meets.

She can't stand men who are detached, and perceives them and her own repressed detachment as deadness, and loss of vitality and the potential for fun.

She has contempt for men who are self-effacing and compliant, just as she finds her own dependency feelings contemptible. She believes that this aspect of herself represents weakness and vulnerability, and she keeps it deeply repressed; but when she meets men who are self-effacing, she sees in them her repressed dependency, and she calls them "nice" but "weak, inconsequential, vulnerable, and unmanly."

She feels that expansive men are strong, virile, interesting, talented—but they steal the show from her. They represent competition and threaten to submerge her own self and to bring her hated, self-effacing trend to the surface.

What can she do?

She can get into treatment and become acquainted with all aspects of her personality. The power and compulsivity of each of her trends must be understood and reduced so that they become accepted without fear. Her externalizations must be understood and reduced. She must clear up muddled feelings and beliefs about weakness, strength, femininity, and masculinity, as well as unrealistic ideas about perfect relating partners. This is no small task. It involves considerable struggle. But it is worthwhile, and Diana has the health, strength, and intelligence to do it.

LEADERSHIP

There is usually a dominant partner in each relationship. However, who that is may not be discernible at first. It is also true that leadership may be shared in various areas of living and that it may also change hands.

Leadership in money, social policy, major familial decisions (medical, educational, economic, and so forth) may look as if it resides in the most expansive person. After all, he or she is most concerned with mastery, while a compliant partner tends to act dependent. But this is not necessarily the case at all.

In some families—and in some business relationships and corporate situations—leadership often falls to the least expert, to the most fragile, and to the most manipulative. Manipulation can be accomplished through martyrdom and the generation of guilt at least as effectively as through bombast and direct domination, and in sadomasochistic interplays both partners contribute their manipulations from either position as they alternate roles.

For example, I know a couple in which the man is strongly expansive and domineering. In my presence, he talks volubly; indeed, he takes over most conversations. She remains as quiet as a mouse and invariably defers to him. But I also know that, despite the man's great appetite for friends and social activity, this couple remains alone for the most part, encapsulated and separate from nearly all community life. Closer investigation reveals that she prefers it this way, and so this is the way it is. Still further investigation reveals that she is the determining policymaker in almost all areas of their lives, despite surface appearances. He is more dependent on her than she is on him, regardless of his overt expansiveness and hidden self-effacement.

Dependency is more often a measure of lack of self-esteem than a question of character structure. Thus, while the expansive person abhors dependency and takes great pride in riding roughshod over his or her relating partner, he will nevertheless be dependent in ratio to his poor self-esteem. And if the self-effacing person's self-esteem is fairly good, he or she may not be dependent on his partner. Submissive, perhaps, but not necessarily dependent. Each type is dependent in his or her own way. The expansive person needs someone to dominate or to sustain his illusion that he dominates. The self-effacing person needs someone to sustain the fact or illusion that he is being cared for. The detached person needs someone to be detached from, to give the fact or illusion of distance. Leadership can fall to any one of these types—whether they lead by producing guilt (self-effacing), bullying (expansive), or staying above it all (detached).

In healthy relationships, leadership resides in the person who is the most skilled and talented in that area. The partner who knows about money assumes leadership in financial decisions. In sick relationships, leadership resides in the most rigid, compulsive, dictatorial, subjective, manipulative, and self-hating person.

To discover the real, rather than the superficial, center of leadership in a relating pair or a given household, look for the person who most influences the general mood of the pair or of the family. The mood of the relating group is an extension of and consistent with the real leader's mood. The real leader will more than anyone else influence the extent to which real feelings are expressed and shared; the degree of open sharing of family information and opinions; how the family functions vis-à-vis the community it lives in. And ask whether this leader leads by virtue of his or her talents, or by virtue of sick manipulation.

TIME AND ACTIVITY

Time is the only thing we are sure of being born with, and the only thing we know we will have spent when we die. What we do with time, in the time of our lives, describes who we are, and the time we spend together tells us something of how we feel about each other. Simply being in another person's physical presence in no way guarantees intimacy, trust, or mutual emotional investment. There are people who spend a great deal of time together—apart. Each may maintain a strict and effective vigil over a self-encapsulation that prevents sharing of anything whatsoever.

Some simple, concrete questions can be quite revealing about a relationship:

Is time spent together avoided? cherished? compulsively diluted by other people or preoccupying activities? How often and for how long can time spent together be exclusive of other people? Does the presence of other people ever feel intrusive? How, when, and how often is time spent together?

Is time spent together used to verbalize real feelings, opinions, ideas, information, or is it characterized by superficial rituals or silence?

Is the activity to which the greatest time and devotion are given a common one or separate? For example, if business absorbs four-fifths of a man's waking time, is his wife an active participant and sharer in that business? If she is not, then he is encapsulated from her. If she is, chances are that the business serves as a vehicle to facilitate shared relating.

Is time spent together followed by good or bad feelings?

Is time used to make claims on each other, to complain, to obsess, to gossip, to attack each other?

How much time can each partner spend alone, without hurt feelings on the part of the other?

How much common interest is there in activities? Are activities freely shared or is there a sense of sacrifice or coercion or complying with necessary duties?

Is occasional preference for other people's company well tolerated, or is it suppressed? Does it lead to reactions of abuse and recrimination?

How much fun is shared together?

Does one person do all the talking? Do neither talk and just spend time together mesmerized by TV?

When the relating pair talk, is the subject of conversation always something apart from the relationship (politics, a new book, the weather)? Is the conversation mainly about *one* member of the relationship? Or equally about the concerns and experiences of both?

Examining what a relating couple does during the course of a week will tell you a lot about that couple, particularly if the time examined is compared to a similar stretch during different seasons and holidays. I remember one man I knew who was shocked by his wife's demanding a divorce after many years of what he fantasized was a wonderful marriage. He was also shocked when a description of their waking time together revealed that it had always been spent in the most vitriolic fights. Indeed, during one vacation trip they came to blows and went home and back to work early. Another woman in a similar situation was surprised to discover that in her "close and loving marriage" she and her husband were spending 90 percent of their time apart.

People who have disparate interests can have a pleasant, constructive relationship, but only if they can pursue their interests guilt-free, without the tyranny of dependency needs, malignant possessiveness, or culturally dictated togetherness.

VI

AFFECTIVE
RELATING

CONSTRUCTIVE AND DESTRUCTIVE OR MALADAPTIVE RELATIONSHIPS

Up until now we have talked about the components of our relationships—the kinds of people we are and the kinds of people we relate to. We have talked about the models our relationships follow and the locks we sometimes put on ourselves and our relating partners. We have explained those forces within ourselves, and those outside ourselves, that influence the way we relate. And we have described the real coinage in which the emotional business of relationships is transacted.

But how can we measure the relative health of our partnerships with others? What interior benchmarks do we use? What do we need for a healthy relationship? What *is* a healthy relationship?

Even the most constructive relationship contains destructive factors, and vice versa. If we speak of a maladaptive relationship, we mean one that is *largely* maladaptive. A healthy relationship is mainly constructive but also has destructive features. This is in-evitable in a society that is largely destructive to human proclivities but that is made up of many individuals whose natural urge is to-ward healthy cooperation.

Most people are aware of being relatively comfortable or un-comfortable in a relationship; excited or bored; liking or disliking; free or stuck; anxious and depressed or fairly happy; jealous, envi-ous, paranoid, or trusting, etc. They seldom think of their relating in terms of health and sickness. They rarely feel responsible for what they come to perceive as destructive.

The most important aspect of *constructive* relating involves freeing each partner's emotions and thus making feelings more available, as well as helping to increase the development and range of each other's feelings.

A maladaptive or *destructive* relationship's deep (not easily discernible) primary characteristic is its stultifying effect on the feelings of the participants. Any force or influence from inside a person or from another person or from society that has the effect of blocking the growth, development, evolution, evolvement, and expression of feelings is destructive. Severely sadomasochistic re-lationships, antagonistic relationships, and some adversary rela-tionships—as we have seen—eventually deaden feelings and destroy spontaneity.

What, then, makes a relationship sick or healthy? Is it always as healthy or as sick as its participants? While this is often the case, it is not always true. As we have seen, poor relating *can* heighten the sick aspects and deaden the healthy ones, making each partner sicker. There are relationships between neurotic people that make the participants behave psychotically to each other, and sometimes to other people, too. This means that these people are much more destructive together than apart.

But sometimes just the reverse takes place: two very disturbed people have a therapeutic effect on each other. Occasionally such pairs can function in the world, provided they are together a good deal of the time, because they need each other in order to make an adequate interpretation of reality. This happens with severely frightened, dependent people who must cling to each other in order to feel enough of a sense of self to function.

There are also people who have a sick relationship together but are relatively healthy when apart. This is not an uncommon situation between some parents and children—the child is felt as an extension of the parent's fragility and vulnerability and the parent is almost paranoically overprotective, although the child is perfectly self-sufficient and the parent, in other contexts, is a relaxed, unapprehensive person. There are also children, middle-aged and older, who are adequately functioning people for the most part, but who—as a result of years of conditioning—become infantile and helpless in the presence of their parents or people who remind them of their parents.

As with most things human, the range of possibilities is enormous: but all relatively healthy relationships—what I call effective or "feeling" relationships—have common characteristics: expression of feelings, wisdom and maturity, an orientation to struggle, an acceptance of deprivation, a tolerance for fair fights, passion, and room for apology and gratitude.

Feelings and Pretense

We come into a relationship already relatively in or out of touch with feelings and with or without strong feelings. Some of us are more repressed, some less; but the relationship itself is expressed through feelings. And the extent to which they are honest, and honestly expressed, is the measure of the success of the relationship.

It is of prime importance to differentiate between authentic feelings and pretended feelings. Pretense and affectation run rampant in our population. Our culture bombards us with messages of how to feel, how to demonstrate those feelings, how to act. So many of us have learned to act so much of the time, we have lost touch with the fact that we are acting or pretending.

But acts and pretense eventually corrode the self and the relating process between selves. Even worse, duplicity and pretense kill trust and establish an atmosphere of apprehension and even paranoia, in which emotions are conveyed through twisted, labyrinthine alleys and almost always have double meanings or implied messages. Sometimes the pretense is shared, and *both* partners are living out a related fantasy. There are, in fact, many people who have constructed intricate, highly embroidered versions of themselves and each other—and in fact these people feel a great deal; but their feelings are related to fantasy rather than reality. The whole structure of their relating lives is based on a mutual idealization that may crumble in an instant should reality come crashing through.

Among honest, real feelings, that of joy—the ability to enjoy each other's company and common experiences—is of vital importance to a relationship. Feeling joy is certainly one of the great human experiential sensations or feelings. But pretense precludes joy, and pretending to be happy is not a relative of real, spontaneous enjoyment. It's either there or it isn't. How do pretense and pride underlying pretense preclude and occlude joy? Joy comes from the real self and is experienced by the real self. It dates back to our earliest gurgling and laughing as free, unpretentious infants. Devoting time and energy to competition or to pretentious self-idealization leaves no time and energy for fun.

We must not confuse competitive victories and vindictive triumphs with joy. The former are the results of temporary victory over others: joy is born of the real self and does not need a competitive, outside reference point. Thus, it is an antidote to sick pride; and our capacity for joy—real joy—measures the degree of our victory over pride.

Joy has two blood brothers—humor and sadness—that are essential to a relationship. Life is tough! Problems—small, large, some of them even insurmountable—are inevitable. The problem is not that there are problems. The problem is expecting otherwise and thinking that having problems is a problem. Tolerating appropriate sadness, being mutually supportive in sadness is very important to a relationship. But in many couples dependency is so great that any sadness or sickness is threatening enough to produce anger and even virtual abandonment. In others, of course, just the reverse is true: trouble brings great mutual support and tapping of strength, resources, and creativity.

The importance of humor cannot be stressed too much. The ability to laugh and to make others laugh is no small matter in providing an antidote to situations that might otherwise turn into chronic, unrelieved states of despair. Humor also bridges impasses in communication and is one of the best mechanisms for preventing and breaking pride deadlocks. Humor helps to dispel artificial and pretentious solemnity. It makes great closeness possible. Having a common sense of humor is almost always evidence of having a common frame of reference in general; and it can help in situations where such a frame of reference is not enough. For while common cultural backgrounds and educational backgrounds help produce commonality of understanding, a common sense of humor can often transcend differences that exist, or it can indicate that seeming differences are really undercut by great similarity in perceptions. I believe this is so because humor often tells us how we make abstractions and react to symbols. It also tells us how we make associations, how one thing reminds us of others. People who have similar capacities to use symbol language, to abstract and to associate, have great ability to communicate both on a nonverbal and on a verbal level. On a verbal level they tend to speak and to understand the same language; on a nonverbal level their responses to events around them are so similar that they seem to have common understanding without speaking and respond as a cooperative team, even as they retain their individuality.

Our culture stresses the importance of how people feel about us—how a lover feels about us. We are inundated with the importance of being liked and admired. But it is how we feel about ourselves and our relating partners that is much more significant. The partner whose presence helps us to generate and to mobilize feelings in us for them is an antidote to loneliness and alienation. Do we empathize, sympathize, revel in our partners' joys and humor? Do we feel for them? Do our feelings come alive for them? This is what caring, investing emotion, and relating are all about.

And the simple fact is that most of us tend to reciprocate. If we call caring—and its constituent feelings and acts of kindness—love, then few of us can experience real love without becoming at least somewhat loving, too. Some people reach these feelings in themselves—neither possessive nor idealistic—with relative ease; others experience them only when they are generated by the presence of a partner. If we have been out of touch with them, our feelings may be abrasive and frightening to us at first, but the sense of aliveness they impart tends to grow in us and to become cherished. So our partner becomes an object of appreciation and love. "I love you" may in large part mean "I love being with you because I love the activated feelings for you which you generate in me; they make me love myself more, too."

The reciprocity of feelings that is the hallmark of a healthy relationship must not be confused with a situation in which couples seem to be *overwhelmed* by feelings for each other. In these symbiotic relationships, if one person is in pain, both moan. Indeed, the boundaries of self seem to be wiped out: both partners function as a single, two-headed human monster. This condition is a result of severe morbid dependency and mutual symptomatology, not of empathy and love.

Real reciprocity of feeling is stimulated by communication: I believe that *telling* helps us to *feel*. We can have feelings—all kinds, including those for each other—without saying anything at all about them. But verbalizing feelings is more than a way of communicating them. It is probably the chief form of exercising them and thereby developing them more fully: from quiet, gentle, and sweet to full, blaring, and tumultuous.

So healthy relating involves *communicating*—of ideas, values, and feelings. We trade feelings, or affect, with our partners, and this exchange brings on still more feelings. This trade, or affect-discharge exchange, is an important and powerful antidepressant, since it works to stimulate feeling; indeed, it is part of any successful therapy between therapist and patient. And it has particular relevance in creative processes. Otto Rank has written about the importance of the artist's partner, supporter, or muse in producing his or her work; perhaps the same process takes place in colonies of artists and in literary circles.

Certainly mutual free-associating about feelings and the creative enterprise springing from this "bouncing off each other" are therapeutic in their enhancement of feelings—and this is the essence of change, growth, and aliveness.

It is important to note that relationships *can* exist at a distance. We can exchange feelings with people even when they are not present. We can have feelings about people we do not know. A troubled young man may fantasize about a relationship with a film star he has never met; his feelings for her may be so strong that he may attempt a violent political act to gain her attention. But I believe that such feelings represent an autistic, narcissistic process; they do not represent the kind of exchange that goes on between real people. Discharge of feelings between real people who are also effecting a real exchange is the stuff of therapy. This can be done via letters or the telephone. But if we consider the range of signals transmitted through body language and even body contact— touch—then the value of being in each other's physical presence is obvious.

Wisdom and Maturity

Wisdom and maturity are almost interchangeable terms when we are discussing relationships. The importance of each to any relating process cannot be overestimated, although they both play a lesser role in minute contact or touch-and-go relationships, among children, among simplistic people, and in shallow, superficial relating. There is no opportunity to be wise in a relationship with one's newspaper dealer or with a so-called friend with whom one has only superficial social dealings.

If I were to differentiate between the two, I'd say that maturity is cognizance of reality and wisdom is acceptance of, or—better yet—the ardent embrace of, reality. As we have seen, illusions may start out as benevolent, protective, and compensatory mechanisms,

but they inevitably turn out to bring on cruel conditions and results—especially in our relationships, where they inevitably lead to
claims, expectations, externalizations, confusion, rage, communication breakdown, displacements, personal unhappiness, anxiety,
depression, and unhappiness with each other.

I've said before and will say again that *life is tough*. Not impossible, but tough. The corollary that follows is that *a price must be
paid*. There is no such thing as a free ride. But people who live on
a relatively high illusionary scale find it very difficult to adjust to
the limitations inherent in the human condition. Their illusions
invariably extend to almost all aspects of life: there is the parent
who believes that children never get sick; the doctor who feels that
all his patients will get well; the speculator who believes that all
his deals will be profitable; the Lothario who will never be rejected;
the athlete who will not lose or be hurt; the parent who believes
that he/she can protect a child from all pain; lovers who feel that
passion will transcend all else and will be consistent and everlast-
ing; on and on it goes. Such illusion must insidiously and relent-
lessly destroy the fabric of relating. Demoralization in facing the
world of reality can only complicate and hurt relationships and
produce a sense of continued impoverishment.

People of maturity, wisdom, and humor negotiate the world
and their lives with compassion and grace, and this makes relating
much easier and more fruitful. They are not stunned by storms of
disillusioning events. Their sense of reality has a cushioning effect,
and their humor helps them through the inevitable tragedy and
loss of life. Perhaps humor helps us to accept some aspects of reality
that would otherwise destroy us in view of our all too human sensibilities; perhaps in this way humor acts as a replacement for illusions.

Illusions about ourselves, our partners, and the process of relating itself are catastrophic to relationships. Living with a self-
deluded person most often means living in a shadow world, full of
bad surprises and misunderstandings. Living with an idealized person invariably leads to disappointment and chronic hostility. Believing that serious emotional relationships occur instantly,

without the benefit of time, work, and struggle, leads to inappropriate and painful matchmaking and to severe disappointment.

Conversely, knowing, *really* knowing, that relationships of a serious nature take time to evolve and to develop is invaluable. Knowing that communication is at best limited is valuable. Knowing that difficulties must ensue in all relationships is wisdom. When partners are not deluded by mutual idealizations but know—really know—each other as real human beings, mutual compassion is possible. And mutual compassion in turn makes relating possible, easier, more enriching to the partners involved—and sometimes just plain fun.

Orientation to Struggle and Deprivation

Obviously, since communication with self involves struggle, communication with another person also involves struggle. Indeed, there is no possibility of relating without struggle, and expectations to the contrary are based on spurious, childish notions about the human condition. But struggle must be differentiated from suffering. From my point of view, one is the absolute antithesis of the other. Neurotic suffering (I exclude suffering imposed on us by forces over which we have little or no control) always exists in the service of self-hate. It is pride-oriented. It says, "Look at me—look how I suffer." Its aim is to produce guilt in the relating partner, or perhaps envy in those not noble enough to suffer equally.

Suffering in a relationship is almost always done to exert one's will over another, often through martyrdom and the generation of guilt. This is the antithesis of the "live and let live" accommodation characteristic of healthy struggle. Struggling, on the other hand, takes place in the service of healthy change and growth. Struggle defines choice. Suffering defines compulsion. Struggle takes time!

One's orientation and willingness to struggle for mutual understanding are major factors in all relationships, particularly in sustained long-term ones. But they are highly subject to cultural influence. Our society undermines the reality of struggle with a message of idealized love. Idealized love implies instant and perfect communication; it denies that there can be any difficulty at all in communication, or that there must be accommodation in all relating, especially that which involves sustained living together. Think of the disappointment this must lead to when we realize it's not true—not to mention the disillusionment with our partners we must feel.

Relationships don't let us off with small adjustments. It is no minor matter to interpret another's language—its particular meanings and special usage, humor, satire, ideas, tastes, needs, desires, goals, moods, and feelings. However, the willingness to undertake this struggle to form bridges of mutual understanding is most important. Without struggle we surely will remain ships that pass in the night.

Accommodation and adjustment are obviously important aspects of the struggle to relate fruitfully. Ordinary give-and-take and the ability to live and let live are not possible without adjustment to individual needs, and especially to each other's limits, problems, idiosyncrasies, sensitivities, and vulnerabilities. To imagine that these do not exist is to ask for serious repercussions, even the destruction of relationships. Even sharing physical things, such as kitchen supplies, bathroom space, living schedules, and responsibilities, requires great adjustment.

Inevitably, there are differences between relating partners, and the struggle to surrender to each other's needs on an equitable basis is surely evidence of relating maturity. When two people have the same conscious priorities and can assert themselves on behalf of these priorities, friction and struggle are minimized. But even highly compatible people can't always synchronize priorities, and a struggle must usually take place involving a trade of priorities. Awareness of this struggle and willingness to engage in it is a measure of the relationship's health. People who place more pride in their principles than in the relationship prefer *suffering* for pride fulfillment to *struggling* for relating growth. People for whom the person is more important than the particular principle that may be involved can more readily struggle for flexible exchange of priorities and preferences.

For example, I know two couples whose personalities are quite similar in that the men place sociability high on their priority list and the women prefer a great deal of privacy. One couple get along quite well: each has struggled to accommodate the other's needs, and they have readily exchanged priorities. The other couple lead an essentially antagonistic existence, are always on the verge of breaking up, feel sacrificed on each other's altar and chronically deprived and put upon. Neither has given an inch in the way of accommodation. Each has suffered on behalf of sustaining personal pride positions. No exchange of priorities has taken place.

We hear the term *incompatibility* so often. There is an incompatibility that refers to lack of mutual sexual attraction. But incompatibility for the most part takes place because of lack of orientation to struggle.

Connected to willingness to struggle is our personal relationship to deprivation. Deprivation is a universal fact of life: it begins the moment we are born and continues all our lives, until we are deprived of life itself. Accommodation, how we adjust and relate to deprivation, begins with the infant's first breath, or perhaps earlier. How we relate to being deprived will determine our capacity for happiness. It is the key to frustration and anxiety tolerance and plays an incalculable role in the formation of disposition and moods. A sunny disposition, for example, is impossible when deprivation is experienced with rage, self-hate, and bitterness.

Deprivation takes place each time a choice is made, inasmuch as we are deprived of the rejected alternative—of work, of food, of time spent in myriad ways, of places to live, of vacations to take. Life simply isn't long enough to do it all. Hierarchies of priorities and choice and living with deprivation are necessary. The alternative is chaos.

One of the main areas of deprivation occurs in the relating process. As we establish relationships, we deprive ourselves of other relationships. We cannot have an infinite number of relating processes going at the same time. In order for a relationship to function at all, at least some minimal surrender must take place. We must, after all, surrender speaking if we are to listen to what a relating partner has to say. We are deprived of privacy each time we communicate an aspect of ourselves.

Any number of choices are good, but in this limited life only a few are possible. Therefore, the reality struggle is not in making the "best" choice but in knowing we must give up something in order to make the choice. Unfortunately, our culture does not prepare us well for this struggle because it constantly drums into us the necessity of having nothing less than everything all the time.

Since the state of being deprived is an ever-present fact of life and is a constant presence in our lives, how we react to being deprived is more important for our relationships than what it is we are being deprived of. A maladjustment to deprivation brings a life of disappointment, cynicism, and even hopelessness and despair to both individuals and couples. It is not unusual to find couples who regard themselves as singled out for deprivation and who live a life of chronic depression. Some of these people become chronic complainers; since they feel especially deprived, they think it is necessary to withhold and to conserve what little they have.

Life is not easy. It forces choices on us, and there are times when we will indeed be deprived—choice and deprivation are for all practical purposes *synonymous*. In a healthy struggle, we face deprivation with equanimity rather than with suffering. Struggle is mandatory if we are to communicate and to relate. Neurotic suffering hinders relating. In essence, the crucial struggle is the process of recognizing, understanding, and putting down one's own pride. This represents the struggle for real self-acceptance and compassion for one's self—compassion for self is invariably translated into compassion for those with whom we relate.

The Approaches to Differences and Fights

If we expect healthy struggle—with ourselves and with our partners—in our relationships, it follows that we should expect differences or disagreements with our partners and that we should consider them a sign of *health*. We must not confuse *differences* with breakdowns in communication and incompatibility. In communication breakdown, a common meeting ground is for the moment precluded or just doesn't exist. This condition is most often due to pride investment and more interest in sustaining pride than in conveying a message. In incompatibility, messages cannot be delivered because there is a lack of common experiences, of similar interests, or of common goals. Communication breakdown is often a temporary condition, but can become extended. Incompatibility is usually chronic and can be remedied only through a prolonged, intensive struggle. Neither can be remedied without great motivation and self-examination.

If we believe that the arrhythmic condition I spoke of earlier is a fact of human life, then we know that the existence of all kinds of differences are inevitable in relationships. Desires, feelings, ideas, positions taken will from time to time be different for each member of a relating unit. In short, partners will not see eye to eye on everything. How they handle these differences is more important than the differences themselves.

A good fight is a good thing—although under ideal circumstances it may not be a fight at all but rather an impassioned argument or dialogue. In a good fight, personal attacks—attacks on each other—do not take place. The fight is about the issue at hand, not about personal triumph over the other person. The attack is against the other person's opinion, but in no way is an attack on the *person* who believes in the different opinion.

At the same time, the most important dynamic of the *good fight* is that nothing is held back. There is minimal suppression (conscious holding back) or repression (automatic, unconscious holding back and putting down out of awareness). There is no residual bad feeling that explodes inappropriately at a later date or is displaced to fuel some form of mutual sabotage. In the good fight, hurting a partner's feelings is not an issue because it is not a goal; therefore, fear of causing pain does not exist and does not create inhibiting effects. Feelings are permitted free flow.

Merrill and Philip disagree about which school their son Tom ought to go to. Philip states his preference, and says why he feels the way he does. Merrill, in turn, states her preference. Throughout their disagreement they remain on good terms, although Philip becomes quite dramatic, loudly telling Merrill how lonely he felt in boarding school and how angry he was at his parents for sending him away. Merrill tells Philip she is terrified of overprotecting Tom by keeping him at home. Many issues are aired, and there is a thorough analysis of which is the best school for Tom. Never does Philip say, "You're afraid of having Tom tied to your apron strings," nor does Merrill attack Philip for weakness and loneliness as a boy. Their "fight" results in a constructive decision, and they feel closer when it's over because they have revealed strong—and vulnerable—feelings to each other.

Merrill and Philip's fight conforms to these characteristics:

1. There are no externalizations or projections.
2. There are minimal or no claims made on the basis of supposed special needs or privileged positions.
3. There are no hampering fears of any kind.
4. Neither wants to punish or to establish superiority.
5. The arguments are issue-oriented and not person-oriented.
6. The arguments are not vindictive, vengeful, or used to score vindictive triumphs.
7. Merrill and Philip are not pride-oriented.
8. The arguments are used to convey opinions, feelings, and information, and there is no winning or losing.
9. The discussion is not followed by abused, martyred reactions, guilt, or feelings related to victory.
10. At least some clarification usually follows, and sometimes changes in opinion also.
11. Concession is not felt as defeat.
12. After the fight, mood is usually elevated.

I think of *good fights* as little fights that occur among *friends*. When no little fights occur, big fights are often the result; these are cumulative explosions, and they can be damaging. But the good fight is an exercise in friendship because free affect discharge and exchange is what being friends is all about. A relationship in which P's and Q's must be watched is a limited, manipulative friendship. Indeed, so much that passes for agreement is really, unfortunately, compulsive compliance masking repressed feelings of disagreement and unfriendly, angry feelings. Effacing of self on the altar of friendship is ultimately destructive to the friendship itself, because there must be a self for one's partner to relate to, especially if the partner is a friend. The willingness and ability of good friends to change and to grow and to become still better friends through good fighting is basic to a relationship, and may well offer one of the most valid measures of friendship.

Passion

As we discussed earlier, the intense explosion of feelings that characterizes infatuations is usually short-lived—and certainly this kind of "passion" has little meaning in a creative, healthy, long-term relationship. Such high degrees of excitation are difficult to sustain, however strong the initial sexual chemistry or idealization of another person may be. And yet many people fear a relationship is "empty" without it. Many wait entire lifetimes for the "right person" to come along and overwhelm them with a passionate burst of emotional idealization. For some it never happens, and they live in a state of semiexcitement mixed with hopelessness, in anticipation and loneliness. For others, to whom it does happen, the explosive feelings of initial infatuation are transformed into the lock of sadomasochism. The relationship is still charged with "passion," but the passion is only a substitute. When it subsides, the relationship often breaks up, because it was based largely on passionate response interplay and little else. Both partners are enormously disappointed to have their expectations of a reciprocally passionate relationship thwarted, and each takes disappointment out on the other.

This early breakup of relationships precludes the longevity a relationship requires if its participants are to achieve a *real* state of sustained passion. For passion *can* be sustained—very strong passion, not at all the same thing as infatuation. This passion cannot take place in grossly immature, undeveloped, shallow people. It cannot take place in highly narcissistic people. It cannot take place in people who don't know each other and who have short-lived relationships.

The passion I speak of here comes from caring. This passion is characterized by very strong, deep feelings for the other person and is experienced sexually. In any case, the feelings involved are almost always therapeutic to the self, producing a feeling of well-being and a kind of inner glow. This passion is not only sustained; it tends to grow and to flourish with the passage of time.

Make no mistake in this regard—I do not mean the obsessive preoccupation with another person that comes from morbid dependency and actually covers up a fear of separation. I mean passion, the real excitement of powerful, alive feelings about the person we care about—passionately—even more than we care about ourselves. While this precludes selfishness and narcissism, it does not call for a morbid, dependent obliteration of self. Quite the contrary. It takes much self—real values, real vitality and contact with inner feelings—to care powerfully and to be full of the passionate joy of caring. It also takes time: time to invest emotionally, to capitulate, to connect, to make history together, to exchange and to care and to be passionate about, in an ever-evolving and self-fulfilling process. The questions here are not "Is she good enough? How does she affect me? How do we fit together? Does she love me?" The questions are "How can I help her? How can I bring joy to her life?"

This kind of caring passion is not born of being loved, nor is it born of inspiration generated by the arrival of an ideal person. It is born of one's ability to love, to actively love another human being without fear of depletion, rejection, attack, or the guarantee of reciprocity. This kind of passionate lover does not love wildly or impulsively or compulsively. His/her love is almost always directed at an equally well-developed human being who also complements the passionate process and makes possible the exchanges of feeling about each other that are the mark of a real and caring relationship.

Functions of Apology and Gratitude

Finally, real and deep relating demands of both partners the ability to know when one has been offensive and to apologize with relative equanimity. The same is true of feeling and expressing gratitude. Neither is to be confused with compulsive or manipulative, unctuous obsequiousness or patronizing, half-masked hostility. I speak here of the real thing only.

I have long felt that humility is one of the most powerful therapeutic forces we have. In relationships, apology and gratitude are the active vehicles of humility. Humility must not be confused with humiliation. One is the antithesis of the other. They are at opposite ends of the pole.

Humiliation is the result of hurt pride. It precludes true apology, gratitude, or forgiveness. It sustains hidden rage and prevents communication. It makes acute problems and their results chronic, lingering conditions and sustains feelings of injustice, abuse, and injury.

Humility is the essence of knowing who we are in both assets and limitations. It is a cornerstone of real self-identity, self-acceptance, and self-esteem. It makes human mistakes acceptable and generates compassion and forgiveness, especially as applied to self. It is the most powerful weapon against pride.

Gratitude and apology are the active extensions of humility as applied to the relating process. Gratitude means serious recognition of kindness, and healthy people appreciate it, not as the narcissist craves admiration and acclaim, nor as the self-effacing person needs to be universally liked, but as a real expression of feeling.

Apology is the best breaker of pride deadlocks. But even more important, it is a symbol and a signal of one's fallibility, limitations, and capacity to err. It is evidence of humanity, and it demonstrates caring about one's partner's feelings and sensibilities. It further indicates that communication and honest relating are more important than sustaining pride positions of perfection, superiority, and arbitrary rightness.

No matter how hard we work at our relationships, no matter how much compassion and real feeling we try to express through them, misunderstandings will occur. We live in an imperfect world, and we are imperfect people. Real apology, real gratitude sustain compassion despite misunderstanding and confusion. They dull sharp edges and soothe raw nerve endings; they prevent recrimination and vindictiveness and help us to achieve an ever-greater harmony with our relating partners.

CONCLUSION

As I have tried to show on every page of this book, how we relate to each other is as important a component of our psychological health as our individual identities are. Destructive relating and destructive aspects of relatively healthy relating twist or blunt our feelings. Repressed feelings can then force themselves to the surface in another form; say, through development of a somatic symptom such as ulcers in a chronically anxious person. Or twisted feelings may be expressed through mutual sabotage, as when one business partner lays traps for the other, all the while seemingly unaware that he feels hostility toward his associate. Blunting of feelings expresses itself as the numbness betrayed by the expressions "I don't know how I feel about it" or "I just don't feel anything about it." In extreme or chronic cases this repression of feelings can result in emotional depression; relationships where the numbing force of repression is less obvious are often characterized as "peaceful" when they are really emotional vacuums. But whenever the relationships between the individuals involved do not permit the free flow of feelings, chronic hopelessness, cynicism, envy, jealousy, possessiveness, fatigue, actual physical complaints, cruelty, recriminations, loneliness, neurotic claims, displacements, projections, frustrations, anxiety, depression, and depletion pollute the lives of the relating partners. And the feeling of depletion can often be felt by people outside the relationship who witness the mutual sabotage of the participants and are themselves drawn into it.

Destructive relationships have an economy of their own, which keeps them going in peculiar balance for years, sometimes even for a lifetime. Feeling unsatisfied or generally unhappy—and the locks that produce those feelings—can become a way of life. The roles determined by our neurotic locks are sustained in part because they have become familiar, and risking unfamiliar territory, however promising of possible happiness, is frightening. Inertia plays an enormous role, particularly in family relationships, and the kind of unhappiness characteristic of destructive relating invariably affects children, who themselves perpetuate their parents' unhappy example in their own lives.

Extrication from the cycle of destructive relating is seldom possible without consciousness and motivation. Many people have been depressed for so long and have related miserably for so long that they are truly unaware of other possibilities. In fact, this lack of awareness, or insensitivity, shows itself in their relating behavior, where ruthlessness, rigidity, polarization, lack of struggle to understand one another, quick formation of pride positions, distrust, and fear often abound.

But this kind of relating activity goes against healthy proclivities in the people involved. As long as any healthy aliveness still exists in either participant, the neurotic lock is threatened by potential attack and collapse—and, as we have seen, the protagonists have to take constant measures to keep the lock locked. Destructive relating—whether it is overtly antagonistic or subtly adversarial—involves much more time and energy than healthy relating. Sustaining rigid, constricted, and even monstrous configurations often requires obsessive preoccupation and total dedication. Sometimes relationships characterized by an unusually high degree of sickness leave no room for other activity or relating. Such relationships sometimes turn into encapsulated, bizarre little worlds with almost no connection to reality.

Healthy relating—cooperative or creative relating—is marked by easy spontaneity. If both participants are not constantly trying to make each other conform to unwritten rules and satisfy unspoken demands, they have more time to devote to the struggle for mutual understanding and growth. If they are not trying to score points off each other, they have more energy for interests and activities *outside* the relationship. This guarantees nourishment from the outside and a more *real* perception of the human condition and the world generally. This kind of relationship lies within the grasp of each and every one of us, if we will just reach out for it. And in reaching out for more open and honest relationships, we will be reaching out for our *selves* as well. For in relating honestly, cooperatively, and lovingly to each other, we open up hidden parts of ourselves to our own view. Just as sick relationships are built on repression, so healthy ones demand—and nourish—openness and spontaneity. As we build more creative relationships with one another, we will be unlocking the best we have to offer ourselves.

VII

EPILOGUE:
A SUGGESTED
THERAPEUTIC
GAME

BASIS OF THE GAME

This is a game to be played by two or more relating partners: husband and wife, lovers, parent and child, friends. Its purpose is to contribute to constructive relating. It is not a simple ventilating exercise; it aims to produce sustained effects of change and growth, to stimulate real insight.

The rules are simple to understand but the game is very difficult to play; and the game requires strong motivation.

The basic rule of the game is that during play the relationship always takes precedence over the individual players.

The game cannot proceed if personal interest is or becomes more important than the relationship itself. It must be remembered that the basic goal is for the relationship to win. Through constructive contribution to the relationship each partner wins. But the purpose of the game must never be converted to a goal—for one partner to *win* over the other.

Any of these elements will impede or even convert the game to a destructive enterprise:

Self-justification
Self-righteousness
Arbitrary rightness
Claims, making demands
Externalizations or blame
Interruptions of each other
Manipulation
Recrimination
Vilification
Guilt or compulsive confession
Feeling abused and bitter
Pride
Concern with being liked
Concern with being admired
Concern with being respected
Inclusion of a nonexpert third party or
    arbitrator, audience, or judge
Application of judgment or moral equivocation
Quest for judgment from some outside source
Condemnation
Expectation of reward or appreciation
Bullying of any kind whatsoever
Conscious lies, willful modifications, or exaggerations

The point of this game is to help us to perceive without judging and to learn from our perceptions. The avoidance of critical judgment is very difficult but extremely worthwhile. It keeps us from letting our emotions distort our perceptions; it also prevents moral equivocations of all kinds, which impede the progress of the game. What the game tries to bring into a relationship is *insight*, not feelings of satisfaction that come from righteous self-vindication.

PROCEDURE

I suggest that the game be played at the same time every day, for no more than twenty minutes at the beginning. Once you feel that you and your partner are in greater tune with each other, the length of time may be increased, but this will probably not happen for at least several months. An attempt to lengthen the time of play before the players are ready usually results in undue fatigue, anxiety, or breakup of the game. However, the twenty minutes must be absolutely uninterrupted by any intrusions whatsoever. You must bring complete (as complete as possible) concentration to the game process.

For ten minutes the two players concentrate on how they can both help one player to elucidate and to remedy any personal difficulty he or she has. Then the concentration shifts to the problems of the other player for ten minutes. "How can *we* help you?" is the crucial question. Not "How can I help you?" "I" is not the same as "we." "We" breaks down the delineating barrier constructively and allows the notion of *us* to enter your life together for a while.

Thus, Alice says to Edward, "Let us both help you." Then, after ten minutes, Edward says to Alice, "Let us both help *you*."

In order to play, Edward must state his problem and take responsibility for it—never trying to put the blame on Alice—and Alice must do the same in her ten minutes. Remember, externalizations, displacements, claims, and self-recriminations will destroy the game!

If Edward says, "I have trouble with you spending money; if I could get you to spend less, I'd have no problem here," he is destroying the game. This is an externalization. It alludes to a problem Alice has. It throws responsibility to Alice. It is designed to produce guilt. It is the antithesis of the game.

If Edward says, "I am frightened about money. I feel that there won't be enough. When money is spent I get angry," he is ready to play the game.

Alice can then say, "Let's explore your fear about money." They both may discuss money and what it means to Edward; what its depletion means to Edward. What the reality of Edward's money situation is, too. They will discuss Edward's anger—perhaps its relationship to fear, especially fear of impoverishment; what he does when he is angry; what he can do when he is angry.

Then, of course, they do the same for Alice. Alice might say, "I feel awful when I have to say no to anyone." Edward must encourage her to explore these feelings, to talk about her need to be liked and her fear of not being universally loved or of incurring other people's anger, and so on.

They must guard against any possibility of judgment or punishment.

They must never use material from the game as weapons against each other, any more than an analyst does with information gleaned from a patient.

During the twenty minutes Edward must not usurp Alice's time or Alice Edward's time.

WHAT DOES
THE GAME DO?

1. It initiates communication.
2. It enhances mutual respect.
3. It exercises feelings.
4. It increases openness and trust, intimacy, and tenderness.
5. It increases empathy and sympathy.
6. It conveys knowledge of each other's real feelings.
7. It increases responsibility for self, for one's own problems, and for the possibility of remediation.
8. It enhances mutual cooperation in establishing a therapeutic relationship.
9. It breaks pride deadlocks and dilutes narcissism.
10. It provides emotional nourishment.
11. Self-hate and hopelessness are diluted.
12. Compassion for self and for each other is enhanced.

WHAT IF NOTHING
COMES UP?

If nothing comes up in the way of a problem, John or Mary may use the ten minutes to talk about his or her pride-invested areas and the problems therein encountered—pride in being strong, in being always right, in sexual prowess, and so on. He or she may explore priorities and feelings about them. He may go over a review of the rules of the game. She may talk about things she would like to do and what she considers self-realizing for her.

Try to say whatever comes to mind—to free-associate for a while—but if the associations are in the form of recriminations, drop them and go on to others. The same is true of claims and what you consider injustices.

Or you might sit quietly and say nothing and, if you are so inclined, hold hands.

CAN EVERYONE PLAY?

E veryone can try. Some people won't be able to play. Their profound alienation, narcissism, pride, rigidity, paranoia, repressed
rage, and immaturity will make it impossible. They will need professional help first. Sometimes a third party, a seasoned player, can
help if he or she is not used as an arbitrator or as a judge to establish
who is right or wrong. His role is to show them how to play.

Where there is an antagonistic relationship, the game cannot
be played unless each player for several months before proceeding
can list at least six personal problems for which his/her partner is
not responsible.

THE GAME AS A PROGNOSTIC INSTRUMENT

Willingness and ability to play the game, rules intact, are indications of a favorable prognosis for your relationship with your game partner.

Inability to play may indicate that the relating process in question may well be in grave jeopardy.

Chronic inability to play may signal that termination of the relationship is in order.

The most common causes of inability to play, suffered by one or both of the participants, may be one or more of the following:

1. Immaturity and lack of development
2. Severe alienation
3. Serious emotional disturbance
4. Intractable externalizations

5. Malignant narcissism
6. Chronic, metastatic neurotic pride
7. Lack of motivation
8. Overwhelming illusions and living in the imagination
9. Overwhelming self-hatred

The presence of any one or more of the above may indicate the need for professional psychoanalytic intervention.

Undergoing treatment when these conditions exist requires great motivation and enormous struggle. Willingness to enter treatment may be viewed as a favorable sign and an indication of some hope for the relating process. But much time and patience are necessary. People suffering from the above difficulties have little experience with struggle or waiting.

WHEN IS THE GAME OVER?

The game is over when ordinary relating and the game are one and the same cooperative process. At this point, we have achieved a creative relating process. The partners derive great satisfaction from participating in each other's self-realization. They care about each other's sensibilities and areas with potential for healthy change and growth. They have an ever-increasing capacity to experience pleasure both apart and together.